To Alt or Not to Alt

Greg Ramirez

Preface

Every story about investments is incomplete without questions, curiosity and a desire to create a future that is secure. The conversation around money usually revolves around a few perimeters: stocks, bonds and maybe some savings tucked away. With the market shifting and the world make its way towards development, many people look beyond the tradition ways of earning and search for something strong, flexible and rewarding. This search leads them to alternate investments.

If you're an everyday investor, a person who saves and a planner, this book is for you! Several stories and real-world examples intertwine to make chapters. They serve as resources that you can use to return to time to time. Whether you

Whether you're new to all this or just trying to get better at it, you'll find helpful tips, simple explanations, and advice that actually works.

Quick riches do not come with promises or easy wins. But it does come with thoughtful exploration and honest assessment. As you move along your journey, you will discover the risks and responsibilities that come with finding possible alternatives to investments. Diversification, patience, and diligence are more than financial buzzwords; they are the backbone of wise investing.

By the end of this journey, you will understand technical details and the mindset that helps investors grow, adapt to situations and protect what matters. My hope is that this book helps you with clarity and spark the confidence to ask, seek out advice and step forward with purpose. Welcome to a new way of thinking about your wealth, one that is build for today's world and a promise for tomorrow.

Contents

Chapter 1: Right Foot In

Welcome to the world of alternative investments!

If you've never heard of them or maybe you have but thought they were just fancy words for something you didn't need to know, ~~don't fret.~~ I promise it's not as complicated as it sounds. By the end of this chapter, you'll not only know what alternative investments are, but you might also start seeing them as a way to make your money work ~~just a little~~ harder for you.

So, What Are Alternative Investments?

Let's start with the basics: alternative investments (or "alts" for short) are just what the name suggests—an alternative to the usual investments you hear about, like stocks and bonds. Think of them as the "odd" investments since they don't follow the typical rules of the stock market. They're like the rebels of the financial world. Stocks and bonds are traditional; they're predictable. They go up, they go down, you buy them, you sell them—end of story. But alternative investments? They live by their own rules.

Alts are not tied to the ups and downs of the stock market, which means when the market is having a bad day (or month, or year), your alternative investments might not be feeling the same pain. It sounds awfully appealing but there's another main aspect that needs to be taken into account beforehand. Alts are often only available to accredited investors, which is just a fancy way of saying you need a net worth of at least $1 million (not counting your primary residence) or an income of $200,000 (or $300,000 if you are married) per year for two years in a row. So, they're a bit exclusive, which can be quite disheartening for a lot of individuals out there who've got their heart set on such investments but do not meet the aforementioned qualifications.

Ultimately, it might be for the best since the burden of not being able to financially recover from an alt that has lost its value may be economically crushing for someone who hasn't got enough to fall back on.

Different Types of Alternative Investments

Now, let's talk specifics. What exactly falls under this umbrella of "alternative" investments?

Well, there are numerous methods of alt investments.

1. Real Estate: We're not talking about buying your neighbor's house and renting it out. Real estate in the alt world can mean anything from large-scale commercial buildings to real estate-backed funds where your money is pooled with other investors to buy something big—like an office tower or apartment complex. These are the kinds of investments where you can almost feel the bricks and mortar under your feet.

2. Private Equity and Venture Capital: This one *sounds* fancy, but in all honesty, it really isn't.

Private equity is just a way of investing in companies that aren't publicly traded on the stock exchange. You know, the ones you've never heard of that are quietly growing behind the scenes. Venture capital is like private equity's cool younger cousin, where you invest in start-ups, hoping that one of them becomes the next big thing. Think of it as buying a piece of the pie before anyone else even knows there's a bakery.

3. Hedge Funds: Hedge Funds have a bit of a reputation. They're known for taking risks and using complex strategies to (hopefully) make big returns. The people running hedge funds are trying to "hedge" their bets to make money whether the market goes up or down. Yes, it can be risky, but it's like any other bet—if you win, you could win big.

4. Commodities: When you think of commodities, think of things like gold, silver, oil, and agricultural products. People invest in these because, in theory, there's always going to be a need for them. Everyone wants gold when the market tanks, and oil isn't going out of style anytime soon, despite efforts to reduce its consumption due to claims its use contributes to climate change. It's not as simple as just buying a bar of gold and sticking it in your closet. There are funds and partnerships that let you invest in these commodities without ever getting your hands dirty (or oily).

5. Energy Investments: Think oil, natural gas, solar power, and wind energy. Some of these are old-school (oil), while others are where the future is heading (solar and wind). You can invest in the companies that produce energy or in funds that are tied to energy projects. Either way, energy is something the world needs to keep running, so there's always money moving in this space.

6. Collectibles: Here's a fun one: sports memorabilia, art, even rare wine—these all count as alternative investments.

Believe it or not, there are people out there making real money from trading baseball cards or investing in paintings. But don't go thinking you'll become a millionaire overnight by buying the next Picasso at a yard sale. These are niche markets where expertise is key.

7. Private REITs and Non-Traded REITs: Let's break this down: REIT stands for Real Estate Investment Trust, which is just a way for you to invest in real estate without having to own actual buildings. With private and non-traded REITs, your investment is tied up for a while (remember, alts are often illiquid), but the idea is that you're in for the long haul and could get some nice returns at the end of it.

Illiquidity: The Price of Patience

Speaking of being in it for the long haul, let's talk about one of the significant characteristics of alternative investments: they're illiquid. In simple terms, it means that you can't easily sell them and get your money back whenever you feel like it. With a stock, you can log into your app, hit "sell," and get cash almost instantly. With alternative investments, not so much. These often come with terms that require you to hold the investments for five years or longer.

Why would anyone sign up for that? Because these investments are designed to grow over time, often outpacing traditional stocks and bonds. Think of it like planting a tree—you don't expect fruit the next day, but give it time, and you might have a whole orchard on your hands. You'll notice this phenomenon come into play quite a few times.

Who Are These For?

Alternative investments aren't for everyone, and the reason behind it is understandable. They're better suited to investors who don't need quick access to their money and can afford to wait for it to grow. If you're close to retirement or already retired, some alts have the potential to provide a steady stream of income, but if you need that money next week for any purpose, these probably aren't for you.

In fact, financial advisors typically recommend that only about 30% of your investment portfolio be in alternative investments. The rest should be in more liquid, traditional assets that you can access quickly if needed. This helps keep a nice balance between risk and reward.

Higher Risk, Higher Reward?

Now, just because these investments are less tied to the stock market doesn't mean they're risk-free. In fact, some may come with more risk, but also the potential for higher returns. It's like playing a higher-stakes game. You're betting on something a little more unpredictable, but if it pays off, the rewards can be well worth the risks. Here's some food for thought from everything we've already discussed in this chapter.

Take venture capital, for instance. When you invest in start-ups, you're essentially putting your money behind an idea that may not even be fully formed yet. Think about companies like Uber or Airbnb. At one point, they were just small start-ups trying to disrupt industries that had been around forever—

taxis and hotels. Now? They're household names worth billions. Early investors who took the risk on these companies saw their investments skyrocket beyond their wildest dreams. But for every Uber, there are plenty of start-ups that don't make it past the first few years. That's the risk you take. Your investment could turn into a jackpot, or it could seemingly vanish into thin air.

Let's shift gears to real estate, another popular alternative investment. Say you invest in a large commercial property, like an office building or a shopping mall. Commercial real estate can provide stable income through rent payments, and if the value of the property goes up over time, you can sell it for a nice profit. Sounds great, right? But here's where the risk comes in: what if the market takes a nosedive, or what if tenants start moving out, leaving empty spaces? Real estate isn't as liquid as stocks—you can't just sell a building overnight. If things go south, you might be stuck with a property that isn't generating income and is worth less than what you paid for it.

To add another layer, consider real estate-backed loans or mezzanine financing (a type of loan). These are riskier because, unlike owning the property outright, you're essentially lending money to someone else with the hope they can repay it, often with interest. If the borrower defaults, you're in a tricky situation. Sure, there might be legal ways to reclaim some of your money, but it's not as simple as cashing out a stock. However, if everything goes according to plan, the returns can be significant, as these types of loans often offer higher interest rates than safer options.

Hedge funds are another classic example of the "higher risk, higher reward" rule of thumb. They are known for using advanced strategies to hedge their bets, trying to make money regardless of whether the market is going up or down. One common strategy is short selling, where the fund essentially bets that a stock will lose value. If they're right, they can make a lot of money, even when the rest of the market is on the decline.

But if they're wrong, it's a different story—remember the GameStop saga? A bunch of hedge funds were shorting the stock, betting that it would fall. Instead, individual investors piled in and drove the stock price up, costing some hedge funds billions in losses. That's the kind of risk hedge funds take—they can be hugely profitable when things go their way, but they can also crash and burn when they don't.

Private equity is another risky player in the alt investment game. When you invest in private equity, you're essentially buying a piece of a company that isn't listed on the stock market. These companies are often under-the-radar businesses that need cash to grow or turn things around. Private equity firms typically buy these companies, try to improve them (or sometimes strip them down to the essentials), and then sell them later at a profit.

The risk is locking up your money for years without any guarantee that the firm can turn the business around. In some cases, the companies might even go under, but when it works, private equity can deliver generous returns. Think of it like flipping a house, but on a much bigger and riskier scale.

One thing that many alternative investments have in common is illiquidity, which we've touched on. Unlike stocks, where you can just hit "sell" and cash out in minutes, many alts require you to hold the investment for years. Let's say you invest in a private REIT (real estate investment trust). These are designed to provide steady income through real estate, but they're not traded on public exchanges, meaning you can't sell your shares whenever you want.

This illiquidity creates risk because life can be unpredictable. You might need access to your cash for an emergency or major purchase, but with an alternative investment, you're stuck for the duration of the investment term—whether it's three, five, or even ten years. You have to be comfortable with the idea that your money is out of reach, potentially for a long time. But because of that longer-term commitment, you often stand to gain more. Real estate, for example, tends to appreciate over time, so by the time you sell, you might have realized a significant return on your investment than you would've had by investing in more liquid assets.

Energy investments can be particularly high-risk, high-reward. If you invest in oil or natural gas projects, you're betting on global demand for these resources. Prices for oil and gas can be extremely volatile, often influenced by geopolitical factors that are completely out of anyone's control. One year, oil prices might soar because of a disruption in supply, leading to huge profits for energy investors. The next year, prices could plummet, and your investment takes a hit.

Renewable energy, like wind and solar, presents its own set of challenges. Sure, the world is moving toward cleaner energy, but it's still a relatively new sector. There are risks involved in investing in the infrastructure needed to support these energy sources, and there's always the possibility that a project could fail due to technological or regulatory hurdles. But if you believe in the long-term future of renewables, the potential returns could be considerable as the world shifts away from fossil fuels.

Another classic alternative investment is commodities, including gold, silver, and agricultural products. Investing in commodities can be seen as a safe haven during economic uncertainty. For example, when the stock market is in chaos, people often flock to gold. The thinking is, "Hey, if the world is falling apart, at least I'll have my gold." Historically, gold has maintained its value over time, making it a good store of wealth when other investments are declining.

But the risk? Commodities can be incredibly volatile. Just because gold has held its value over the long term doesn't mean there won't be wild swings in the short term. The same goes for agricultural products like wheat, corn, or soybeans. Prices for these goods can be affected by things like weather patterns, trade wars, or shifts in global demand. You could see huge gains in one year if there's a shortage of wheat due to a bad crop season, but you could also face losses if the market suddenly gets flooded with supply.

Investing in collectibles like art, rare coins, or even sports memorabilia can be both exciting and risky. Imagine buying a painting for a few thousand dollars, only to have its value skyrocket to millions because the artist becomes famous. That's the dream scenario. However, for every Picasso, there are countless pieces of art that are not appreciated much over time. The art world is notoriously unpredictable, and values can fluctuate wildly based on trends, the artist's reputation, and market demand.

When it comes to sports memorabilia, the same can be true. You might pick up a rookie baseball card for a few hundred dollars, only to see its value soar if that player becomes a legend. But there's no guarantee. You're betting on market demand for something that, in the end, is just a piece of cardboard or a shiny metal disk. It's a passion-driven investment, often based on the whims of collectors.

Ultimately, alternative investments are about balancing the potential for higher rewards against the increased risks. The key is to only allocate a portion of your portfolio to these high-risk, high-reward investments. I recommend that my own clients limit their alternative investments exposure to about 30% of their portfolio. This way, they can pursue those bigger returns without jeopardizing your entire financial future if things don't go as planned.

For those willing to take on the risk and ride out the longer holding periods, alternative investments can be a powerful tool for growing wealth. Just remember—while the reward can be higher, the risks are real, and not every bet will pay off. It's about finding that balance between caution and ambition.

The Benefits of Diversification

One of the main reasons people like alternative investments is that they add diversity to a portfolio. Imagine you have all your money in stocks and bonds, and then—boom—the market crashes. Ouch, right? But if you had some alternative investments in the mix, like real estate or private equity, those might be doing just fine while the rest of the market is going haywire.

Diversification means not putting all your eggs in one basket, and in the investment world, that can be a lifesaver. Alts, because they don't move in lockstep with the market, can help smooth out the bumps. So, while your stock investments might take a hit, your real estate or energy investments might still be chugging along.

Tax Advantages

Now, for something we all want for our earnings, savings, and assets, paying fewer taxes on them. Some alternative investments come with tax advantages that can be a game changer for people with a higher net worth. Many alts issue what's called a K-1 tax form, which reports things like income and dividends. The nice part? K-1s can come with tax perks, like allowing you to defer taxes or reducing your overall tax bill. Instead of getting taxed right away on income (like you would with a 1099), some of these investments let you wait until you sell to pay the IRS.

This is especially appealing to wealthier investors who don't want extra taxable income every year. It's less about how much money you make and more about how much you get to keep.

Chapter 2: Rethinking Risk and Reward

Visualize yourself at a buffet, surrounded by dozens of dishes to choose from. Would you load your plate with just one item, or do you try a little bit of everything to get a well-rounded meal? Well, most of us would probably go for a mix, hoping that if one dish isn't that great, the others will make up for it.

Investing works in much the same way, and that's exactly what Modern Portfolio Theory (MPT) is all about – creating a "portfolio" of investments that balances risk and reward. Tracing its history, it was introduced in the 1950s by Harry Markowitz, and quickly transformed the world of investing by emphasizing the benefits of diversification, or spreading your money across different types of investments. This theory has become a starting point of financial planning, helping people pass through the often-unpredictable routes of investing.

Instead of just trying to pick the "best" individual investment, MPT focuses on how different investments interact with each other in a portfolio. It's like building a team: you don't need a group of identical players; you need people with different strengths who work well together. MPT encourages us to look at the big picture, combining assets that react differently to market changes, so that when one investment is down, another might be up, smoothing out the overall ride. It's this balancing act that makes MPT such a powerful tool, whether you're saving for retirement, looking to grow your wealth, or just aiming to protect what you already have.

Let's dive deeper into what MPT is, why it's essential for financial planning, and how it's different from the traditional approaches that have been around for years.

The Modern Portfolio Theory

Modern Portfolio Theory, or MPT, is a way of thinking about investing that aims to find the "sweet spot" between risk and return. Suppose you have a certain level of risk you're comfortable with, maybe you're okay with a few bumps along the way, but you don't want any wild swings. MPT helps you build a portfolio that aims to get the highest possible return for that level of risk. It's based on the idea that by mixing different types of assets, like stocks, bonds, real estate, and other investments, you can reduce the overall risk in your portfolio without necessarily sacrificing potential returns. Each asset class reacts differently to economic events, so when one is struggling, another might be doing well, which helps stabilize your portfolio. It's more or less about building a balanced team.

Importance of MPT in Financial Planning

So why should you care about MPT? Well, whether you're just starting to invest or you've been at it for years, MPT provides a solid framework for making smart investment choices. Instead of jumping on trends or picking stocks at random, MPT encourages a strategic approach that considers both your goals and your comfort with risk. Let's say you're investing for retirement, and you have a long-time horizon. MPT can help you create a portfolio with a mix of growth-oriented assets, like stocks, and safer investments, like bonds or cash equivalents. Or, if you're nearing retirement, MPT might guide you toward a portfolio that emphasizes stability and income over high returns, so you're not caught off guard by market downturns.

Using MPT in financial planning helps you think ahead, so you're not just reacting to market changes but planning for the long term. It allows you to create a diversified portfolio that fits your unique situation and evolves with you as your financial goals and risk tolerance change. By understanding the trade-offs between risk and return, you can make decisions that align with what you want to achieve, whether it's growing your wealth, preserving capital, or generating income. MPT makes it easier to keep your eye on the prize, without getting too rattled by the market's ups and downs.

The Traditional 60/40 Portfolio Model

If you've ever sat down with a financial advisor or researched basic investing strategies, you've probably heard about the "60/40 portfolio." This is one of the most well-known, time-tested approaches to investing, and for good reason. The idea is simple: you put 60% of your money into stocks and 40% into bonds. The thinking behind this is that stocks, which are a bit more volatile, can give you the growth you need over time, while bonds, which tend to be more stable, provide stability when the market gets unstable.

For decades, the 60/40 model was a primary feature in financial planning, offering a solid balance of risk and reward. Stocks generally have higher growth potential but can be unpredictable, while bonds are seen as safer and more dependable. Together, they form a portfolio that allows investors to experience growth without being overly exposed to risk. This approach works especially well for people who don't want to get too hands-on with their investments. It's reliable and fairly easy to manage, making it a popular choice for a "set it and forget it" approach to investing.

Limitations of the Traditional Approach

However, as good as the 60/40 model sounds, it's not without its drawbacks. For one, the world of investing has evolved since this approach first came on the scene. Today, sticking strictly to stocks and bonds can leave you vulnerable to certain risks. When the stock market crashes, even the bond portion may not always be enough to offset losses, and bonds don't provide the same level of income they once did due to historically low interest rates. Additionally, bonds no longer offer the yield they once did, making them less effective as an income source. In times of high inflation, for example, both stocks and bonds can struggle, meaning your portfolio may not grow as much as you need it to over the long haul. This shift away from high-yield bonds has led investors to seek alternative options that can provide better downside protection and lower volatility.

Another limitation is that the 60/40 model doesn't take advantage of the wide array of investment options available today. In a world where there are so many diverse asset classes, like real estate, private equity, and interval funds, sticking to only stocks and bonds can feel a bit like relying on an old-fashioned helping kit in a high-tech world. These additional asset classes can provide extra layers of diversification and, in some cases, even more stability, which the traditional 60/40 split just can't offer. For investors who want more flexibility and customization in their portfolios, the 60/40 model can feel a bit outdated. Moving beyond stocks and bonds can offer enhanced downside protection and reduce volatility, appealing to those seeking a more balanced approach.

A lot of younger people, especially millennials, are more interested in alternative investments, leaving behind the 60/40 model. They've seen times when the stock market hasn't performed well, so they're looking for options beyond just stocks and bonds. With the understanding that bonds no longer yield what they once did, they're more open to alternatives that can offer more stability, diversity, and better income potential in their portfolios.

Why Many Financial Institutions Still Use This Model

So, if it has limitations, why do so many financial institutions still promote the 60/40 portfolio model? The answer is partly tradition and partly simplicity. The 60/40 model has been around for a long time, and it's familiar to both investors and financial advisors. It's easy to explain, easy to set up, and relatively low-maintenance, making it appealing for people who want a straightforward investment strategy. For many institutions, it's a go-to model for clients who don't need a lot of customization or who are looking for a simple way to balance growth and security.

Plus, the 60/40 model still works for certain types of investors, particularly those with a moderate risk tolerance who aren't interested in a lot of investment complexity. It provides a baseline approach to balancing risk and return, and, for some, that's all they need. However, as markets continue to change and more asset classes become accessible, many investors are exploring new strategies that go beyond the 60/40 model. So, while this traditional model has its place, it's worth considering whether a more modern, diversified approach might be a better fit for your financial goals today.

For example, consider the Alaska Permanent Fund, which manages the state's oil revenues. The fund doesn't just stick to stocks and bonds; it allocates its investments across various asset classes, including global equities, real estate, and private equity. This diversified approach has allowed the fund to maintain stability and even continue making payouts to Alaskans, despite the ups and downs of the market.

Similarly, the Ontario Teachers' Pension Plan invests in everything from infrastructure to commercial real estate and private debt, helping to secure the long-term future of the pension fund. These funds have moved beyond the traditional 60/40 model, applying MPT principles to build portfolios that are more resilient and better equipped to handle economic shifts.

Advisors on Call's Approach to Portfolio Allocation

At Advisors on Call, we believe that building a portfolio is about more than just choosing stocks and bonds. It's about creating financial assistance that can handle whatever uncertainty you may encounter. That's why we recommend a diversified approach that goes beyond the traditional 60/40 split, aiming for a more flexible and robust strategy. Our recommended allocation includes 30% in equities, 30% in alternatives, 20% in insurance, and 20% in interval funds. This mix allows us to balance growth, stability, and flexibility, providing a more adaptable portfolio tailored to your unique needs and goals.

Think of it like putting together a puzzle. Each piece represents a different asset class with its own purpose: equities for growth, alternatives for income and stability, insurance for safety, and interval funds for liquidity. Together, they form a complete picture that helps you reach your financial goals while managing risk more effectively than a traditional portfolio might. With our diversified model, you're not just relying on two types of investments; you're tapping into a broader range of options that work together to create a well-rounded strategy.

Benefits of a Diversified Model Compared to the Traditional 60/40

Why go beyond the 60/40 model? The answer lies in the power of diversification. By incorporating different asset classes, we're able to spread risk more effectively. Instead of putting all your eggs in one basket, you're spreading them across a range of investments that each react differently to market changes. This means that when one part of the market is down, another part of your portfolio may be up, helping to smooth out the ride. With our approach, you're not just balancing risk and reward—you're also opening up new opportunities for growth and income that the traditional model might miss.

Our diversified model allows us to adjust your portfolio according to your risk tolerance and financial goals. For example, if you're comfortable with a bit more risk, we might increase the equities portion to give you more growth potential. Or, if you're looking for more stability, we can add to the insurance or interval fund allocations. The flexibility built into this model means we can create a portfolio that's truly customized to you, not just a one-size-fits-all solution.

How Different Asset Classes Are Utilized for Various Investment Goals

Our recommended allocation isn't just a random mix; each asset class plays a specific role in helping you reach your goals:

Equities: Equities, or stocks, are the growth engine of your portfolio. They offer the potential for higher returns, which can help you build wealth over time. Stocks also serve as a hedge against inflation, which means they can help preserve your purchasing power as the cost of living rises. By allocating 30% to equities, we're positioning a portion of your portfolio for growth, helping you stay ahead of inflation while aiming for long-term gains.

Alternatives: When we talk about alternatives, we're looking at assets that don't necessarily follow the ups and downs of the stock market. Think of private equity, real estate, or even commodities. These investments provide a buffer against market volatility, helping to protect your portfolio when stocks might be having a rough time. With 30% in alternatives, you're getting both downside protection and potential income opportunities that can add stability to your financial strategy. Alternatives are like the anchor of your portfolio, giving you a solid base that's less influenced by market swings.

Insurance: The 20% we allocate to insurance isn't just about safety; it's about providing guaranteed income and security for the future. Insurance products can offer dependable income streams, which can be especially valuable during retirement. Many insurance options also come with long-term care benefits, which can be accessed tax-free if needed for healthcare expenses. This allocation gives you a reliable safety net, ensuring that a portion of your portfolio is protected against life's uncertainties.

Interval Funds: Interval funds offer liquidity with flexibility. They allow for withdrawals on a quarterly or annual basis, providing access to your investments without the need to cash out in a hurry. With 20% of your portfolio in interval funds, you have a financial resource that's accessible yet stable, offering an additional layer of flexibility. Interval funds are unique because they can hold a mix of assets, like real estate or debt instruments, that don't fluctuate with the stock market.

This adds another level of diversification to your portfolio while giving you access to funds when you need them.

In combining these asset classes, we're creating a portfolio that doesn't just aim to grow but is also prepared to weather market ups and downs, offer steady income, and adapt to your changing needs over time. It's a proactive approach that helps you make the most of your investments while keeping risk in check. By understanding and utilizing the unique strengths of each asset class, Advisors on Call can help you build a financial foundation that supports your goals, now and in the future.

The Role of Interval Funds in a Modern Portfolio

Interval funds are a special type of investment that combines both stability and flexibility. Unlike traditional mutual funds, interval funds aren't traded on the stock market every day, so you can't buy or sell them whenever you want. Instead, they work on a set schedule, allowing you to buy or redeem shares only at specific times, like every quarter or once a year. While this setup might seem, a bit limiting at first, it actually has some great benefits, especially for keeping a portfolio steady during the ups and downs of the market. Interval funds provide more control, making them a useful addition to a diversified investment strategy.

One key difference between interval funds and mutual funds is how they handle liquidity—meaning, how quickly you can access your money. With mutual funds, you can buy or sell shares on any day the market is open, giving you quick access to your cash. Interval funds, on the other hand, offer access to your investment only during certain windows. Although this may not be ideal for short-term needs, it can actually add stability over the long term. Since they're not traded daily, interval funds are less affected by the day-to-day market swings, which makes their performance more consistent. This can be especially appealing if you're looking to reduce volatility in your portfolio.

Interval funds typically invest in alternative assets like commercial real estate, private loans, and debt instruments—things that don't usually move in sync with the stock market. These assets are chosen because they can provide steady income and stability over time, even when traditional markets are going through tough times. For example, an interval fund might include a mix of real estate properties or business loans, giving you the chance to earn income from assets that aren't heavily influenced by the daily market ups and downs. By including these types of investments, interval funds open up opportunities that you wouldn't usually find in regular mutual funds or other common investments.

The benefits of interval funds become clear when you see how they fit into a balanced portfolio. First, they don't follow the stock market too closely, so their value doesn't swing as much with stock price changes. This makes them a great way to diversify, adding stability to your overall investment strategy. Second, their scheduled liquidity gives you more access than some other types of alternative investments, allowing you to withdraw your funds at regular intervals without locking them up for years. Finally, interval funds can work with different risk levels; they can be set up to focus on income, growth, or a mix of both, depending on the assets included in the fund.

In short, interval funds bring flexibility, reduced volatility, and access to unique investments to a portfolio. By holding them alongside traditional investments like stocks and bonds, you're adding an extra buffer that can help smooth out the ride when the market gets bumpy. With interval funds, you're not just getting another type of investment—you're gaining a tool that combines income potential, scheduled access to your money, and added protection to help keep your portfolio strong over the long run.

Expanding Beyond Bonds: Alternative Investments

When we talk about alternative investments, we're looking at a world of possibilities that goes beyond the usual stocks and bonds. These investments are like the "wild cards" of a portfolio—assets that don't necessarily follow the ups and downs of the stock market. That's what makes them so valuable. Alternative investments are typically less correlated with traditional markets, meaning they often move independently of the stock market. This characteristic can help balance out a portfolio, providing stability when stocks are struggling and offering new avenues for growth and income.

Let's break down some of the most popular types of alternative investments.

1. **Real Estate (Commercial & Residential):** Real estate is one of the most popular ways to invest outside of stocks and bonds. It includes both commercial properties (like office buildings and shopping centers) and residential ones (like apartment buildings). When you invest in real estate, you can earn money through rental income and possibly see the

value of the property go up over time. Since real estate is a physical, tangible asset, it doesn't respond to stock market ups and downs like other financial investments. For instance, an office building in a great location can continue to generate rent, no matter what's happening with the stock market. On top of that, real estate offers tax benefits, like the ability to deduct depreciation and other expenses, which can help you save money on taxes.

2. **Debt Instruments (Mezzanine Financing):** Debt instruments, such as mezzanine financing, are another interesting option. Mezzanine financing is a type of loan that sits between regular debt and equity. It's a high-risk loan that can still give the lender returns, even if the business doesn't perform well. Because it's riskier than traditional loans, mezzanine financing typically offers higher interest rates, giving investors a way to earn more income. Sometimes, it also provides a small equity stake in the company, so if the business does well, the investor can share in its success. Since these investments aren't closely tied to stock market changes, they can help diversify your portfolio.

3. **Private Equity and Distressed Asset Funds:** Private equity involves investing in private companies that aren't on the stock exchange. This could mean supporting a startup, helping an established business grow, or buying a struggling company and turning it around. Distressed asset funds specifically invest in companies that are in financial trouble but could recover with the right help. These investments can lead to big returns because you're buying at a discount and profiting from the company's improvement. Although private equity

usually requires a long-term commitment, it offers access to high-growth opportunities that aren't available in public markets.

4. **Natural Resources (Gas and Oil):** Investing in natural resources like gas and oil is another way to add stability to your portfolio. These resources are essential to the economy, and their demand tends to stay steady, regardless of stock market changes. In addition to earning potential returns through dividends or revenue sharing, gas and oil investments can come with tax benefits. For example, there are deductions for things like exploration and development costs, which can lower your taxable income. Since these resources are more connected to the overall economy than the stock market, they provide another way to diversify and manage risk in your investments.

Tax Advantages and Considerations in Alternative Investments

One of the most appealing parts of alternative investments is the tax breaks they can offer. For example, real estate and gas and oil investments often allow deductions for depreciation and operating expenses, reducing your tax bill. Private equity and certain debt instruments might also benefit from lower long-term capital gains taxes. However, each type of alternative investment has different tax rules, so it's important to work with a tax advisor to make sure you're getting the most tax-efficient benefits for your portfolio.

In short, alternative investments like real estate, mezzanine financing, private equity, and natural resources can be valuable for a balanced investment strategy. They allow you to tap into unique opportunities, gain potential tax benefits, and reduce your exposure to the ups and downs of the stock market. By exploring these options, you can build a stronger, more diversified financial plan.

Customizing Portfolio Models Based on Risk Tolerance

When building a portfolio, one of the most important factors to consider is risk tolerance. Risk tolerance is essentially how comfortable you are with the ups and downs of the market. Some people can handle a bit of turbulence, while others want a smoother ride. Understanding your own risk tolerance is crucial because it shapes your entire investment strategy. At Advisors on Call, we take the time to assess each client's risk tolerance through conversations, questionnaires, and financial reviews. From there, we can design a portfolio that aligns with your comfort level while working toward your goals.

Age, market conditions, and personal goals also play a big role in shaping a portfolio. Younger investors with longer timelines might lean more toward growth-oriented investments since they have time to recover from market dips. Meanwhile, those closer to retirement often prefer a portfolio that emphasizes stability and income to avoid unexpected risks. Changing market conditions and specific financial goals, like buying a home or planning for retirement, also influence how we allocate assets. For example, during periods of market uncertainty, we might increase exposure to alternatives that don't correlate with stock market movements, like real estate or private debt.

We offer different portfolio models tailored to each level of risk tolerance. For the more risk-averse, a conservative portfolio might include a higher allocation to bonds, insurance products, and stable alternative assets. Moderate investors may have a balanced mix of equities, alternatives, and income-focused investments, providing growth potential while managing risk. For those with a higher risk tolerance, a growth-oriented portfolio could allocate more to equities and higher-yield alternatives, allowing for more significant growth opportunities.

Liquidity Considerations and Rebalancing

Liquidity, or how quickly you can access your invested funds, is a crucial consideration when incorporating alternative investments into a portfolio. Unlike stocks and bonds, which are easily tradable, alternatives like real estate or private equity often have longer lock-up periods, meaning your money may be tied up for months or even years. That's why we carefully assess your liquidity needs before deciding on the right mix. For instance, if you need access to funds in the short term, we may include more liquid alternatives like interval funds that offer regular withdrawal opportunities.

Rebalancing is another critical part of managing a diversified portfolio. With traditional investments, rebalancing is typically done once or twice a year to keep your portfolio aligned with your goals. However, with alternative investments in the mix, we often take a more customized approach.

Alternatives don't fluctuate with the market in the same way as stocks, so they don't require frequent adjustments. We actively manage the public market side of your portfolio, making regular adjustments to the stocks and bonds based on market conditions and performance. Periodically, we also assess the alternatives to ensure they're performing as expected and remain aligned with your financial strategy.

Fiduciary Responsibility and Client-Centric Approach

At Advisors on Call, we take our role as fiduciaries seriously. As fiduciaries, we're legally and ethically committed to acting in your best interest, not ours. This commitment goes beyond simply managing your money—it means taking the time to understand your goals, educating you on your options, and making recommendations that align with your unique situation. Our client-centric approach ensures that your needs come first, and we're here to provide guidance and support at every step of your financial journey.

Sometimes, our clients come to us with specific investment ideas that may not align with their risk tolerance or financial goals. In these cases, we work together to find solutions that meet their desires without compromising their portfolio's stability. For example, a client may want to invest in a high-risk asset for the chance of substantial returns. If we feel this isn't suitable, we'll explain the potential risks and explore alternative options that offer growth while staying within their risk tolerance. By balancing your interests with our professional judgment, we create a strategy that aims for both growth and peace of mind.

Alternative Investments as Growth and Protection Tools

Alternative investments are more than just tools for diversifying a portfolio—they can also play a dual role in growing and protecting wealth. For clients who are conservative and prioritize stability, we often include alternatives like real estate and fixed-income private debt. These assets provide steady returns and are less impacted by stock market volatility, making them ideal for wealth preservation. With a conservative strategy focused on alternatives, we aim to safeguard your portfolio while offering potential income.

For those looking to grow their wealth, alternative investments provide unique opportunities. While stocks are traditionally associated with growth, certain alternatives, such as private equity and distressed asset funds, offer similar (or even greater) potential for appreciation. These types of investments allow you to tap into markets not available to the general public, often leading to higher returns.

Whether the market is up or down, alternatives can help you weather both stable and volatile conditions. In stable markets, they contribute steady income and incremental growth. During downturns, they can act as a protective barrier, as their performance often isn't tied to the stock market. This makes alternatives a powerful tool in a well-rounded portfolio, enabling you to build wealth over time while providing a cushion against the unexpected twists and turns of the market.

Real-World Client Success Stories

I'd like to share a couple of stories from clients who have successfully used alternative investments to improve their financial outcomes. These examples highlight the unique advantages that these investment strategies can offer, from tax savings to better returns. They're real stories that illustrate how making thoughtful adjustments can lead to significant positive changes.

Example 1: Business Owner Saving on Taxes Through Fee Simples and Gas/Oil Investments

A successful business owner was looking for ways to lower their tax burden while still maintaining a diversified portfolio. After exploring different investment options, the owner was introduced to alternative investments, including fee simple real estate ownership and gas and oil investments. Fee simples, which grant full ownership rights over a property, allowed the client to benefit from property depreciation and other deductions. Meanwhile, investing in gas and oil opened the door to further tax advantages, such as deductions for exploration and development costs.

These alternative investments not only helped the business owner save significantly on taxes but also provided steady income from rental properties and potential gains from energy investments. The strategy allowed the client to maintain a strong portfolio with solid growth prospects while also benefiting from tax efficiency.

Example 2: Former CD Investor Shifting to Alternatives for Better Returns and Tax Savings

Another client, who had previously been a conservative investor, primarily relying on certificates of deposit (CDs), began to feel frustrated with the low returns offered by these traditional investments. The client sought alternatives that could offer higher returns without taking on excessive risk. They were introduced to private equity opportunities and mezzanine financing, which provided higher potential returns compared to CDs.

The client made the transition and saw significant improvements. Private equity investments, in particular, allowed them to invest in fast-growing companies, while mezzanine financing offered a steady income with a higher interest rate than their previous CDs. Additionally, the tax benefits associated with these alternative investments further increased the client's overall returns, making the switch to alternatives a smart financial move.

Key Takeaways from These Client Transformations

These two examples highlight some of the significant benefits of alternative investments:

1. Tax Savings: Both clients were able to take advantage of unique tax benefits associated with alternative investments. Fee simples, gas/oil investments, and real estate provide opportunities for tax deductions and deferrals that are not available with more traditional investments.

2. Higher Returns: Shifting from traditional investments like CDs to alternatives such as private equity and real estate allowed these clients to achieve better returns, helping them grow their portfolios more effectively.

3. Diversification: These alternative assets provided additional layers of diversification. By moving beyond stocks and bonds, clients were able to spread their risk across different asset classes, reducing their exposure to market volatility.

4. These stories show how taking a customized approach and exploring alternative investment options can lead to improved outcomes. By understanding your goals, risk tolerance, and current financial situation, you too can discover strategies that help you save on taxes, increase returns, and strengthen your overall financial position.

Suitability of Alternative Investments

Alternative investments can open up some exciting opportunities, but they're not available to just anyone. There are a few eligibility requirements, and it's all about making sure these investments are a good fit for each investor. Generally, you need to meet certain financial criteria to qualify as an "accredited investor." This usually means having a net worth of at least $1 million (not counting your primary residence) or earning an annual income of $200,000 individually, or $300,000 with a spouse, over the last two years. This rule isn't there to exclude people but to make sure anyone investing in alternatives has the financial stability and understanding to handle the risks involved.

Aside from eligibility, alternative investments also tend to come with higher minimum investment amounts than your average stock or mutual fund. Many of these investments require a minimum of $25,000, while some might start at $50,000 or even $100,000. It all depends on the type of asset and the specific opportunity. For example, private equity funds or commercial real estate projects often need larger sums because they're longer-term and involve more complex structures like partnerships or limited liability companies (LLCs). These structures allow multiple investors to pool their money together, share in the profits, and benefit from the assets' potential growth.

The Future of Diversified Portfolio Management

Looking ahead, it's easy to see that diversification is a smart strategy that can make a real difference. By including alternative investments in a portfolio, we're able to smooth out some of the bumps that come with traditional stocks and bonds. Alternatives like real estate, private equity, and natural resources bring in income, offer unique tax advantages, and help balance out risk. A well-diversified portfolio has the power to weather market ups and downs while still working to grow your wealth and keep you on track toward your financial goals.

At Advisors on Call, we're always evolving our strategies to keep up with the times and meet our clients' needs. The world of investing doesn't stand still, and neither do we. As new opportunities arise and markets shift, we stay on top of the latest options and adjust our approach to reflect current trends.

By being adaptable, we can continue offering customized, thoughtful investment strategies that suit each client's goals. We're committed to giving you a mix of assets that not only suits today's financial nature but is also prepared for whatever tomorrow might bring.

The Learning Curve

However, before you go rushing to invest in that alternative energy fund or buy shares in a hedge fund, remember this: alternative investments are complex. They often come with a steep learning curve and you need to do your research (or maybe work with someone who has either done the research or is experienced in it). You want to make sure you're getting involved with reputable investments and managers who know what they're doing.

Fiduciary advisors (these are people legally obligated to act in your best interest) can help make sure you're investing wisely. Not all financial advisors deal with alternative investments, and those who do should be able to explain the risks and rewards clearly. If they can't, maybe it's time to find someone else.

Two great examples of good strategy when it comes to this are Harvard and Yale. Both are renowned for their successful endowment strategies, which have consistently delivered strong returns over the years. These strategies are particularly notable for their significant allocation to alternative investments. The universities emphasize a diversified portfolio, spreading investments across various asset classes. This includes traditional assets like stocks and bonds, as well as alternative investments such as private equity, hedge funds, real estate and natural resources.

This means that a substantial portion of their portfolios is dedicated to alternative investments. Yale's endowment has been a pioneer in this area, with a significant allocation to private equity, real estate, and hedge funds. Harvard follows a similar approach, aiming to reduce risk and enhance returns through diversification. Both endowments employ active management strategies, leveraging the expertise of skilled investment managers to identify and capitalize on opportunities in the market.

To conclude, understanding alternative investments—how they work, how they differ from one another, and how they fit into your overall strategy—is essential to building a strong, diversified portfolio. These investments serve a variety of purposes: some aim to reduce risk by offering protection from the volatility of public markets, while others provide unique opportunities for growth or tax advantages. However, without a clear grasp of their structure and purpose, investors risk making choices that don't align with their goals. Careful consideration is key—because with alternatives, the right strategy can offer long-term value, but the wrong fit can set you back.

Chapter 3: To Alt or Not to Alt

For a moment, close your eyes. Suppose you hear the word "Investing," what pops up in your mind? For many, I believe, there must be stocks and bonds! However, alternative investments, or "alts," offer an interesting twist by bringing in options beyond these traditional assets. Alts can sometimes feel a bit unconventional, but they serve a solid purpose: they offer ways to invest that don't necessarily follow the usual stock or bond market swings. Because they're often less connected to the market's day-to-day ups and downs, they can add a layer of stability to your portfolio, helping cushion it against sudden changes in traditional markets.

This brings us to why alts are so valuable in diversification. The idea behind diversification is to spread your investments across different types of assets so that your whole portfolio doesn't take a hit if one area suffers. By adding alts into the mix, you're widening your options and potentially lowering your overall risk. If stocks are down, alts might stay steady or even perform well, balancing out some of the volatility and reducing the impact on your overall portfolio. In short, alts can help create a more resilient investment plan.

Including alternatives in a broader portfolio strategy isn't just about adding variety; it's about creating balance. Every type of asset brings something unique to the table. For instance, stocks offer growth potential, bonds add stability, and alternatives introduce benefits like downside protection and additional income opportunities. Through combining these different assets, you can build a portfolio that's well-prepared for various economic scenarios and tailored to different financial goals.

When we look at alternatives, they often add value by providing protection against market downturns and offering growth in ways that might not be possible with only stocks and bonds. They can work alongside traditional assets to reduce the "all eggs in one basket" risk and potentially increase returns over the long term. So, rather than viewing alts as just an optional addition, consider them a smart ingredient in a well-rounded portfolio built to adapt and grow through different market conditions.

The Role of Alternatives in Portfolio Diversification

While building a portfolio, one of the key goals is to create a stable, resilient structure that can withstand market ups and downs. This is where alternative investments come into play. Unlike stocks, which can be prone to significant swings in value, many alternatives are less affected by daily market changes. This "non-correlation" means that if the stock market experiences a sharp downturn, some alternative investments may stay steady or react differently. As a result, alternatives can act as a safety net for your portfolio, helping reduce overall volatility and potentially protecting against large losses when markets fluctuate.

Think of it this way: instead of putting all your eggs in one basket, alternatives let you place some of those eggs in baskets that aren't so easily shaken by the stock market's ups and downs.

Income Stream: Consistent Returns Without Market Dependence

Another unique feature of certain alternative investments is their ability to provide steady income. Unlike stocks, whose dividends and values are closely tied to market performance, some alternatives generate returns that don't fluctuate with market swings. Real estate investments, for example, might provide rental income, while certain types of private debt or dividend-yielding assets can deliver regular payouts regardless of how the broader market is performing. This can be particularly valuable if you rely on your investments to generate an income stream - whether to support your retirement or supplement your earnings, because it adds a level of reliability.

Imagine a situation where the stock market takes a hit, causing many portfolios to drop in value. With income-generating alternatives, you can maintain a steady flow of income even in such situations. For those who want to avoid major disruptions to their cash flow, alternatives can be an attractive option, helping to provide a sense of financial security that isn't entirely tied to the market.

Clarification: Not All Alternatives Are Income-Generating

It's important to note that while many alternatives can provide stable income, not all of them are designed for that purpose. Some alternatives are focused on growth rather than income generation. For instance, private equity investments or venture capital funds are typically growth-oriented - they involve investing in companies that are expected to grow over time, with the potential for larger returns down the line. However, these types of alternatives may not provide regular payouts, as they aim to build value over a longer period and often involve higher risks in exchange for potentially higher rewards.

In short, alternatives aren't a one-size-fits-all solution. Some may be perfect for creating a stable income stream, while others are geared toward long-term growth and potential gains. Knowing the purpose of each alternative investment is essential to understanding how it can fit into and benefit your overall portfolio strategy. So, whether you're seeking steady income or aiming for growth, there's likely an alternative investment that can help you achieve your specific financial goals.

Types of Income-Generating Alternative Investments

When looking for ways to generate a stable income outside the usual stock market options, certain types of alternative investments can be a game-changer. These investments offer consistent returns, making them appealing to anyone seeking regular income without relying solely on traditional dividends or bonds. Let's explore some of these income-generating alternatives and see how they might add value to a diversified portfolio.

Private placements are investments that allow individuals to put their money into companies or projects without going through public markets like the stock exchange. These can include investments in private companies, real estate developments, or even specific industries like energy or technology. Since private placements aren't publicly traded, they offer investors a chance to earn income from unique sources that aren't easily affected by day-to-day stock market fluctuations.

The income from private placements usually comes in the form of interest payments or distributions. For example, if you invest in a private real estate project, you might receive regular payouts based on the rental income from that property. Although private placements can offer high returns, they are often intended for accredited investors, as they carry higher risk and typically require a longer-term commitment. But for those who qualify and are looking for income that's independent of the stock market, private placements can be an appealing option.

Moving forward, preferred stocks are a hybrid investment, combining elements of both stocks and bonds. They provide investors with a fixed dividend - meaning you'll receive regular payments, much like a bond, without being as sensitive to market fluctuations as regular stocks. Because preferred stockholders get paid dividends before common stockholders, they're often considered a more secure investment. This priority can make preferred stocks especially attractive if you're seeking steady income, as the dividends tend to be reliable and predictable.

Unlike bonds, preferred stocks can offer some growth potential, as they may increase in value over time. However, they aren't as volatile as common stocks, so they tend to offer a middle ground. For anyone looking to blend the advantages of stock and bond investing, preferred stocks can be an effective way to achieve a steady income stream while still participating in the market's potential for growth.

Real Estate Investment Trusts, or REITs, are a popular choice for investors looking to earn income through real estate without the hassle of directly managing properties. REITs pool money from multiple investors to invest in income-producing properties, such as apartment buildings, shopping centers, office spaces, or warehouses. By law, REITs must distribute at least 90% of their taxable income to shareholders as dividends, making them an attractive option for anyone looking for regular income.

When you invest in a REIT, you benefit from the income generated by these properties, usually through rent payments or property appreciation. Since REITs are publicly traded, they offer a level of liquidity that many other alternative investments don't, allowing you to buy and sell shares as easily as you would with stocks. This flexibility, combined with the steady income REITs provide, makes them a great choice for investors who want exposure to real estate but prefer a hands-off approach. With REITs, you can participate in the potential growth and income of real estate without needing to worry about property management.

Each of these income-generating alternative investments - private placements, preferred stocks, and REITs, offers unique benefits and can add a valuable source of regular income to your portfolio. They provide ways to diversify and let you earn consistent returns, making them an ideal fit for anyone looking to create a more resilient and well-rounded investment strategy.

Characteristics and Returns of Income-Generating Alternatives

Alright so, now when it comes to income-generating alternatives like REITs and preferred stocks, a key attraction is the regular dividends they offer, which can provide a steady cash flow. Unlike traditional stocks, which may or may not pay dividends depending on a company's performance, these alternative investments are often structured to deliver consistent payouts on a predictable schedule. Let's dive into the types of returns you can expect and the different ways these investments handle payouts.

Example Dividends for REITs and Preferred Stocks

Let's follow an example; some REITs provide quarterly dividends that range from 8-9%, depending on the type of real estate they invest in and their overall performance. This means that for every $1,000 invested, you might earn around $80-$90 per year, paid out in quarterly installments. Similarly, preferred stocks can yield high returns, with some options paying 8.3% or even more in monthly dividends. This structure provides regular income and also makes budgeting easier for investors who rely on these funds.

It's worth noting that certain structured alternatives; such as private placements or specialized income funds, may offer even higher rates. Some options are designed to deliver initial returns of 10% or more, making them particularly attractive for those looking to boost their income. However, higher yields often come with longer holding periods or higher risk, so it's essential to evaluate these factors before diving in.

Payout Structures and Timing: Quarterly vs. Monthly Dividends

One of the unique aspects of income-generating alternatives is the variety of payout structures they offer. Many REITs and preferred stocks pay dividends on a quarterly basis, which means investors receive payouts four times a year. This setup works well for those who want to receive steady cash flow without too much frequency, making it easier to track and reinvest dividends if desired. Quarterly payouts are also beneficial for those who prefer a more traditional payout schedule, as they align well with many financial planning strategies.

On the other hand, some alternatives, like certain preferred stocks, offer monthly dividends. Monthly dividends can be especially appealing if you're looking for a more frequent income stream to cover regular expenses, such as bills or rent. For investors who rely on their portfolio for monthly cash flow, these options provide a smoother and more predictable source of income, allowing them to better manage their finances. However, it's essential to remember that the frequency of payouts doesn't necessarily impact the total annual return; it's simply a matter of when and how often you receive it.

Each alternative investment comes with its own specific payout structure, so understanding how often you'll receive dividends can help you choose the best option for your financial goals. Whether you prefer quarterly or monthly payouts, REITs and preferred stocks offer flexible solutions, allowing you to enjoy a steady income that can complement other sources of revenue in your portfolio. This flexibility, combined with the potential for higher returns, makes these income-generating alternatives an excellent choice for investors seeking consistency and growth.

Assessing Client Needs for Alternative Investments

Investing in alternative assets like private placements or certain hedge funds often requires meeting specific financial criteria, known as "accreditation requirements." To be an accredited investor, you typically need to have a net worth of at least $1 million (not counting your primary residence) or an annual income of $250,000 (or $300,000 for joint filers) over the past two years. These requirements are in place to ensure that individuals investing in potentially high-risk alternatives have enough financial stability to handle the associated risks. Essentially, regulators want to make sure that investors are well-prepared and financially secure enough to handle the ups and downs that can come with these types of investments.

For non-accredited investors, those who don't meet the $1 million net worth or income criteria, the options for alternative investments are generally more limited. While there are still some alternative investments available for non-accredited individuals, they tend to have lower returns and fewer choices, focusing on safer, more regulated options. However, this doesn't mean that non-accredited investors are left out; there are still ways to diversify and achieve steady income through traditional assets or specific REITs and interval funds designed for the general public.

Factors in Determining Suitability: Finding the Right Fit

When it comes to deciding if alternative investments are a good fit, several factors ought to be considered. One of the most important is risk tolerance; how much uncertainty and fluctuation in investment value an investor is comfortable with. Alternative investments can be more volatile or have longer holding periods than traditional stocks and bonds, so understanding an investor's comfort with risk is key. Age can also be a factor; for instance, younger investors may have a higher risk tolerance and longer time horizon to absorb potential losses, while older investors may prioritize stability and steady income.

To tailor alternative investments to individual needs, advisors often use an investor questionnaire. This questionnaire assesses various factors such as financial goals, investment preferences, risk tolerance, and timeline. With this information, advisors can recommend a portfolio that fits the client's unique situation. For example, if a client has a high-risk tolerance and a long-term growth goal, they may be steered toward growth-oriented alternatives. Conversely, a client with lower risk tolerance and an income-focused goal might be directed toward income-generating alternatives like REITs or preferred stocks. This personalized approach ensures that clients' investments align with their financial goals and risk preferences.

Clients Interested in Alternatives: Working with Advisors for Specialized Expertise

Some investors prefer to take a hands-on approach when it comes to traditional stocks and bonds, managing their portfolios independently. However, alternative investments often require more specialized knowledge and access, which is why many of these clients choose to work with advisors specifically for their alternatives. Alternative investments can involve complex structures, regulatory requirements, and market dynamics that are difficult to navigate without experience. By working with an advisor who has a unique expertise in alternatives, these clients gain access to investment opportunities that aren't available to the general public, along with guidance on which options best suit their needs.

This hybrid approach, where clients manage their core portfolios on their own while leveraging an advisor's expertise for alternatives, can be ideal for those who enjoy being actively involved in their investments. It allows clients to maintain control over their main assets while benefiting from an advisor's in-depth understanding of alternative options. This way, they can achieve a diversified portfolio with access to potentially lucrative opportunities in alternative markets without needing to become experts themselves.

Economic and Personal Factors in Alternative Investment Decisions

When you find yourself considering alternative investments, it's important to think about more than just potential returns. Both the broader economic environment and personal circumstances can play a big role in determining which investments make the most sense. Here's a closer look at how these global, domestic, and personal factors influence alternative investment choices.

Global and Domestic Economic Conditions: The Bigger Picture

The world we live in is increasingly interconnected, and events on a global or domestic scale can significantly impact investment decisions. For instance, a looming recession or geopolitical conflict can cause volatility in certain markets while potentially creating stability or growth in others. During times of economic uncertainty, like a recession, we might want to steer clear of higher-risk international alternatives and instead look at domestic options that tend to be more stable. On the other hand, when global economies are thriving, diversifying with some international alternatives can provide higher returns and broader exposure.

What if there's a slowdown in international markets but the domestic economy is performing well? In that case, we might decide to focus more on domestic alternatives, such as real estate investments within the U.S., rather than international real estate or emerging market options. Essentially, keeping an eye on these larger trends helps ensure that our investments are well-positioned to weather changes in the economic landscape, making our portfolios more resilient no matter what the future holds.

Personal Economic Factors: Tailoring Alternatives to Your Life Situation

Economic conditions aren't just about what's happening on a global or national level; our personal financial circumstances also play a huge role in how we invest. For instance, if you're currently employed and have a steady income, you may be more comfortable taking on alternative investments with a longer holding period. However, if you're in a situation where your income is less certain, say, you're between jobs or planning to retire soon, then flexibility becomes more critical. In these cases, we might look for alternatives with a quicker return or more liquidity, so you have easier access to funds if needed.

This approach helps ensure that your investments align with your personal economic stability. If you're in a phase where you're focusing on income generation, such as retirement, income-producing alternatives like REITs or preferred stocks might be ideal. But if you're still in the growth phase of your career and building wealth, you might lean towards alternatives that focus on long-term growth, like private equity. Through considering personal circumstances, we're not just investing in alternatives for the sake of diversification; we're creating a portfolio that supports your specific life goals and financial security.

The economic environment is constantly shifting, and sometimes those changes bring unique opportunities. For instance, when interest rates are high, certain alternative investments; like fixed-income private placements or debt instruments, can provide attractive returns compared to other options. Or consider the impact of the COVID-19 pandemic: while it created global market instability, it also led to new investment opportunities, especially in industries like technology and healthcare that thrived under lockdown conditions.

Why do you think adaptability is so important in alternative investing? Mainly because it allows us to take advantage of economic trends as they emerge, maximizing returns in favorable conditions and adjusting strategies when the landscape changes. Staying flexible doesn't mean we need to chase every new opportunity, but it does mean being open to reevaluating our approach when external conditions present potential advantages.

Direct vs. Indirect Investment in Alternatives

There are two primary ways to get involved in alternative investments: through direct investments or indirect investments. Each has its own set of benefits and risks, and understanding the difference can make a big impact on your investment experience and outcomes. Let's break down how they work and what to keep in mind when choosing between them.

Direct investments in alternatives are made with the help of a fiduciary, like a Registered Investment Advisor (RIA). Fiduciaries are legally bound to act in your best interest, which is especially important when surviving the complex world of alternative investments. With direct investments, an RIA or other fiduciary conducts thorough due diligence on each opportunity, examining the investment's legitimacy, risks, and potential returns. This careful vetting process provides confidence that you're investing in regulated, compliant assets, reducing the risk of scams or hidden issues.

For instance, if you're looking at investing in a private placement or a real estate project, your advisor will verify the legitimacy of the company or property and ensure it's in good standing with the SEC (Securities and Exchange Commission). This kind of oversight can offer peace of mind, especially since alternative investments can be more complex and less transparent than traditional assets like stocks or bonds. By working directly with a fiduciary, you're gaining access to high-quality opportunities that are aligned with your financial goals and are held to strict regulatory standards.

Risks of Indirect Investments: Caution with Unregulated Paths

Indirect investments, on the other hand, can carry significant risks, especially when you're dealing with unlicensed intermediaries or "middlemen" who might not have your best interests in mind. These intermediaries may offer you access to alternative investments but lack the licenses and regulatory backing to guarantee a secure and transparent process. Without proper oversight, indirect investments can lead to issues like excessive fees, unclear terms, or, in the worst cases, outright fraud. Some intermediaries may sell investments that sound promising but haven't gone through the rigorous checks required for compliance, leaving investors vulnerable to unforeseen risks.

An example might be an unregulated "advisor" selling shares in a real estate project that hasn't been vetted for compliance or legitimacy. Without regulatory checks, you could end up putting money into a project that's poorly managed or even non-existent. For these reasons, it's crucial to make sure any indirect investments are compliant with SEC standards or, better yet, to avoid them altogether if there's any doubt about their legitimacy. The lack of due diligence and regulatory oversight in these types of investments can lead to unexpected losses, so it's worth sticking to reputable paths.

Why Regulatory Compliance Matters

When investing in alternatives, regulatory compliance is essential. Alternatives often come with higher stakes and longer commitments, so it's critical that each investment meets industry standards for transparency and security. For instance, SEC-compliant investments provide documentation, disclosures, and legal safeguards that help protect investors' interests. Without this compliance, investors are left vulnerable to unregulated practices that may prioritize the seller's gain over their security.

In short, if you're considering alternative investments, it's wise to work directly with a fiduciary or RIA. These professionals bring expertise and due diligence to each investment, while ensuring that your interests are protected by legal and regulatory frameworks. This level of protection and professionalism makes a world of difference, especially in an investment landscape where the stakes can be high. So, whether you're looking to diversify with private equity, real estate, or other alternative options, choose direct investments with an advisor who can help you navigate the opportunities securely.

Appropriate Allocation of Alternatives in a Diversified Portfolio

Finding the right balance for alternative investments in a portfolio is like fine-tuning an instrument; too much of one thing can drown out the rest, while the right mix creates harmony. When it comes to alternatives, there's a standard recommendation that financial advisors often follow: cap these investments at about 30% of a client's liquid net worth. This cap isn't a rigid rule, but it's a useful guideline for ensuring that we keep liquidity and flexibility in mind.

Standard Allocation: Why 30%?

So why is 30% a sweet spot for alternatives? Unlike stocks or bonds, which you can generally buy and sell quickly, many alternative investments require a longer commitment. Certain alternatives, like private equity or real estate partnerships, can have holding periods of four, five, or even seven years. By keeping the allocation at around 30%, we're making sure that enough of your money is still easily accessible if you need it. Life can be unpredictable, and we don't want to lock up more funds than you're comfortable with for an extended time.

In addition, limiting alternatives to this percentage allows the remaining 70% of the portfolio to stay flexible and liquid. This gives you plenty of room to make adjustments or access funds without disturbing your alternatives. This balance between growth opportunities in alternatives and liquidity in other investments like stocks or bonds helps maintain a healthy portfolio that can adapt to your needs as they change.

Reasons for the 30% Cap: Balancing Long-Term Gains with Accessibility

One of the primary reasons for the 30% cap is to avoid excessive lock-in of funds. Many alternative investments are designed to deliver returns over the long term, which is fantastic for growth potential but can be a drawback if you suddenly need cash. Imagine investing 70% of your net worth in alternatives, only to realize a few years down the line that you need access to those funds for an emergency or a big opportunity. You'd be stuck with limited options to pull from, and in most cases, alternatives can't be liquidated quickly without taking a loss.

The 30% cap also makes sure that other asset classes, such as stocks, exchange-traded funds (ETFs), or insurance products, are readily available for immediate liquidity needs. These other investments are easier to sell or convert to cash if necessary, allowing you to access funds without touching your alternatives. In this way, alternatives can do what they're meant to - grow wealth over the long term - without putting your immediate financial needs in jeopardy.

Portfolio Diversification: Creating Balance Across Asset Classes

A well-diversified portfolio includes more than just stocks and bonds. Through integrating alternatives, stocks, interval funds, and insurance products, you create a balanced portfolio that's designed to perform well under various market conditions. Alternatives add a layer of protection, often performing differently than traditional assets, which can reduce volatility. Meanwhile, interval funds offer periodic liquidity, acting as a middle ground between the easy access of stocks and the longer lock-in of alternatives. Insurance can also provide benefits like guaranteed income, giving you another stable source of funds.

This mix diversifies your risk and manages cash flow. If the stock market drops, your alternatives may still hold steady, providing a buffer that can soften the blow to your portfolio's overall value. If you need quick cash, your liquid investments in stocks or ETFs can provide that, keeping your alternatives untouched and able to grow as intended. Ultimately, this combination of asset classes works together, creating a strong foundation that supports both short-term needs and long-term financial goals.

Impact of Alternatives on Portfolio Management and Rebalancing

When managing a diversified portfolio, adding alternative investments changes the game a bit. Alternatives often require a long-term commitment, so while they can bring stability and unique returns, they also make portfolio management and rebalancing a little more nuanced. Let's explore how alternatives impact the way we manage and adjust our portfolios over time.

One of the defining characteristics of alternative investments is their long-term nature. Unlike stocks or bonds, which you can typically buy and sell at will, many alternatives; such as private equity, real estate partnerships, or certain structured products, require holding periods that stretch over several years. When you invest in alternatives, you're often in it for the long haul, which means we can't just move them around whenever the market shifts or your financial goals evolve.

This long-term commitment influences how we approach rebalancing. While we might frequently adjust stocks or other liquid investments to keep your portfolio on track, alternatives are more of a "set it and forget it" component. Instead of selling or shifting alternatives when the market changes, we'll focus on rebalancing the more flexible parts of your portfolio. Think of your alternatives as the foundation of a building: they're steady and largely untouched, while we adjust other assets around them to ensure the entire structure remains strong.

Managing Other Portfolio Assets: The Importance of Liquidity

Because alternatives are less liquid, it's crucial to maintain a balance of liquid assets, like stocks, ETFs, and even interval funds - alongside them. These liquid assets provide flexibility, allowing us to make adjustments when needed and access funds in case of unforeseen expenses or opportunities. If your portfolio were entirely tied up in long-term alternatives, it would be challenging to adapt quickly or raise cash when needed.

Having liquid assets is essential for regular rebalancing, too. Over time, as certain investments perform better or worse than others, the balance of your portfolio shifts. For instance, if stocks have a great year, they might start taking up more space in your portfolio than we originally planned. By rebalancing, we can "trim" those gains and move funds to other areas to maintain your target allocation. Liquid assets give us the flexibility to make these adjustments, allowing your portfolio to grow while staying true to your risk and return goals.

Alternative Assets in Rebalancing: Finding the Right Balance

With alternatives holding steady in the background, rebalancing focuses on the liquid parts of your portfolio. But that doesn't mean alternatives are ignored; they're still part of the overall picture. When we rebalance, we consider how your alternatives fit into the broader strategy, making sure they complement the rest of your portfolio. For example, if we notice that your interval funds or equities have grown significantly, we might rebalance by allocating a portion of these gains to alternative investments if the timing aligns with your goals and market conditions.

In some cases, the performance of your alternatives might impact how we adjust other assets. For instance, if your alternative investments are generating strong returns and meeting your income needs, we might shift more of your equity allocation toward growth-focused stocks. Or, if alternatives are providing enough stability, we could allocate a bit more to higher-risk opportunities, knowing that your alternatives provide a solid foundation.

Client Success Story: Growing Wealth with a Balanced Portfolio

Visualize starting with a relatively conservative portfolio, one focused on stable, low-risk options like annuities and certificates of deposit (CDs). That's exactly where David Miller began, with a net worth of about $1 million, investing primarily in these safer, steady-return assets. This approach offered him a sense of security but limited growth, as annuities and CDs generally provide modest returns that don't always keep up with the pace of inflation or align with David's long-term wealth goals.

After a thoughtful discussion about his financial objectives, David expressed an interest in growing his wealth more actively. Working together, we explored moving beyond traditional investments to include alternative assets, like real estate and private placements, as part of a diversified portfolio. Through carefully blending these alternatives with traditional equities, interval funds, and even some insurance-based products, we designed a portfolio that balanced security with enhanced growth potential. Over the next few years, this diversified mix protected David's initial capital and also grew his net worth from $1 million to $1.8 million - an impressive increase achieved through the strategic addition of alternatives.

Client Satisfaction: Embracing a Long-Term View with Steady Returns

One of the most rewarding aspects of this approach was the client's satisfaction with the consistent, steady returns they enjoyed over time. Shifting from a conservative, low-growth portfolio to one that included alternatives meant that, rather than relying solely on the predictability of annuities and CDs, the client now benefited from assets designed for growth. But instead of feeling the anxiety that sometimes comes with new investment types, the client embraced a long-term perspective. Rather than tracking daily or monthly fluctuations, they focused on annual performance, allowing the portfolio to grow naturally over time without the stress of short-term market changes.

The client quickly found value in this approach, appreciating that their wealth was not only secure but actively working for them in a way it hadn't before. As they saw their net worth increase each year, they gained confidence in their diversified portfolio and the balance it struck between growth and stability. This success story illustrates how a well-rounded approach - one that combines traditional assets with alternatives - can offer a meaningful boost to a portfolio, allowing clients to pursue their financial goals with greater confidence, patience, and satisfaction. The steady, reliable gains demonstrated to the client that with a strategic blend of investments, they could achieve substantial growth while still enjoying peace of mind.

Options for Clients Interested in Alternatives but Retaining Their Current Advisor

For many investors, alternative investments are a compelling way to diversify and potentially increase returns. However, some clients already have an advisor they trust for traditional investments and may not want to disrupt that relationship. Fortunately, there's a flexible option: the dual advisor strategy. This approach allows clients to work with multiple advisors—one who specializes in alternative investments and another who focuses on traditional assets like stocks, bonds, and mutual funds. By bringing in a second advisor, clients can benefit from the expertise needed for navigating alternatives without changing their current setup.

A dual advisor strategy can offer the best of both worlds. The original advisor continues managing the traditional part of the portfolio, while the new advisor brings specialized knowledge and access to alternatives like private equity, real estate, or structured products. This way, each advisor works within their area of expertise, ensuring that each part of the portfolio is professionally managed and tailored to meet specific goals.

Structuring Portfolios with Separate Advisors for Cohesive Management

While having two advisors might sound complicated, with clear communication and coordination, it can be a seamless experience. Think of it as building a team with complementary skills. Both advisors need to understand your overall financial objectives, risk tolerance, and timeline so they can structure your investments cohesively. By aligning both advisors' strategies, you ensure that your portfolio remains balanced and that each investment supports your long-term goals.

For example, the traditional advisor may focus on growth through equities and income through bonds, while the alternative investment advisor adds assets that bring stability and non-correlated returns. Each advisor may review your portfolio periodically, making adjustments based on the other's moves, so that all pieces work together harmoniously. Communication is key here; regular check-ins with both advisors allow them to stay in sync, avoid overlap, and keep your investments aligned with your objectives. This structured, coordinated approach allows clients to retain the advisors they trust while accessing a wider range of investment options.

The dual advisor strategy provides a unique solution for those interested in the benefits of alternative investments but wanting to maintain continuity with their primary advisor. It allows clients to explore a diversified investment path with specialized support for alternatives while preserving the trusted relationship they already have for traditional investments.

Importance of Fees and Costs in Alternative Investment Recommendations

When considering alternative investments, it's essential to keep an eye on fees and holding costs. While alternatives can be a fantastic addition to a portfolio, the costs associated with them can vary widely. Let's explore how fees work in this realm and why understanding them can make a big difference in maximizing your returns.

One of the advantages of working with a fiduciary for alternative investments is that fees and holding costs tend to be relatively minimal. Fiduciaries, like Registered Investment Advisors (RIAs), are obligated to put your interests first and often work with low-cost, transparent fee structures. In many cases, the primary expenses you'll encounter with alternative investments managed through a fiduciary are custodian fees - charges by the institution that holds your investments. These custodian fees are typically modest and ensure the safe handling and maintenance of your assets.

Because alternatives often require longer holding periods, it's reassuring to know that these holding costs are predictable and won't chip away significantly at your returns over time. Working with a fiduciary gives you the benefit of clear, straightforward fees, which can make a long-term commitment to alternatives feel more manageable.

Indirect vs. Direct Costs: The Hidden Expenses of Indirect Investments

Not all alternative investments are created equal when it comes to costs. Direct investments in alternatives, such as those made through a fiduciary or RIA, generally carry fewer and more transparent fees. In contrast, indirect investments; often sold through intermediaries who may lack the licensing and regulatory oversight of fiduciaries, can come with higher costs and additional risks. These intermediaries might charge higher fees or markup investments, which can quickly eat into your returns without offering much additional value.

Let's say you're interested in a private real estate investment. If you go through a fiduciary, you might pay straightforward custodian fees and management fees if applicable. However, if you're dealing with an indirect investment through an unlicensed intermediary, you could end up with extra layers of fees that aren't immediately apparent, like additional sales charges, marketing fees, or even hidden costs that reduce your returns. Understanding these differences is essential, as indirect investments can sometimes look appealing but actually lead to a lower net return once all fees are factored in.

Cost-Efficiency in Alternatives: Maximizing Returns with Low Fees

One of the main reasons investors are drawn to fiduciary-managed alternatives is the cost efficiency these options provide. Fiduciaries aim to keep fees low and transparent, which means you're less likely to encounter unexpected costs that could impact your returns. When the primary expenses are limited to essential costs; like custody fees or occasional management fees, more of your money is working toward generating returns instead of being absorbed by fees.

The potential for strong returns combined with relatively low fees makes fiduciary-managed alternatives particularly attractive. Over time, even small differences in fees can add up, significantly impacting your overall gains. With fiduciary-managed alternatives, you know exactly where your money is going and can feel confident that you're getting a good value. This cost-efficiency allows you to fully benefit from the growth potential that alternatives offer while keeping expenses under control.

In the end, being mindful of fees and costs ensures that you're maximizing the value of your alternative investments, ultimately helping you achieve your financial goals with greater confidence and transparency.

As we wrap up, it's clear that alternative investments can add real value to a diversified portfolio. By including alternatives, you're broadening the potential for steady income, reducing risk through non-correlated assets, and opening up avenues for growth that go beyond traditional stocks and bonds. These investments bring a unique balance; while stocks may fluctuate and bonds may offer modest returns, alternatives like real estate, private equity, or structured funds can provide the kind of stability and income stream that helps a portfolio stay resilient. For many investors, alternatives are an effective way to weather market ups and downs while keeping their portfolio aligned with long-term financial goals.

However, one must be mindful of the fact that investing in alternatives isn't a "one-size-fits-everyone" kind of choice. Choosing the right alternatives requires careful assessment, taking into account both the broader economic landscape and individual client needs. Economic factors, like interest rates and market conditions, can influence which alternatives make sense at any given time. For instance, a high-interest-rate environment might make certain debt-based alternatives more appealing, while a strong real estate market could be ideal for adding REITs. At the same time, we need to consider your specific financial circumstances, your risk tolerance, time horizon, and personal goals. For instance, a younger investor with a high tolerance for risk might benefit from growth-focused alternatives, while someone nearing retirement may prioritize income-generating investments for stability.

Chapter 4: Pros and Cons of Investing in Alternatives

Alternative investments, once mainly reserved for large institutions and high-net-worth individuals, are increasingly making their way into the portfolios of everyday, or retail, investors.

This shift is largely due to the growing number of platforms, resources, and products that simplify access to these types of investments. Real estate, private equity, hedge funds, and commodities, all considered alternative investments, are now options for individual investors who seek to diversify beyond traditional stocks and bonds.

However, as with any type of investment, it's important to look beyond the initial appeal and understand that alternative investments come with their own set of complexities. Nothing in the world of investing is purely positive or negative; each approach has both potential benefits and possible drawbacks.

Alternative investments may offer opportunities for growth and diversification, but they can also present certain risks. Just as these investments can add value to a portfolio, they can also introduce new challenges, making it essential for investors to fully understand how they fit within their overall financial strategy.

Now that you have a basic understanding of alternative investments, let's take a closer look at both the positive and negative sides of these options.

Pros of Investing in Alternatives

Unlike traditional investments, alternatives often have unique characteristics that set them apart. They are typically less liquid than stocks or bonds, meaning they may be harder to sell quickly. However, this long-term focus is also what can make them valuable in a diversified investment plan. They're often used by investors looking for different ways to grow wealth, beat inflation, and add a layer of security through diversification. Because they tend to respond to various economic factors, alternative investments can offer flexibility and resilience, allowing investors to protect and potentially grow their assets in unique ways. Let's dive into the advantages of investing in alternative assets in detail.

Portfolio Diversification

When it comes to investing, one key idea stands out: don't put all your eggs in one basket. That's where portfolio diversification comes in, and alternative investments play a special role in achieving it. But what makes alternatives such strong diversifiers?

First, let's break down what we mean by "diversification." In simple terms, diversification means spreading out investments across different assets to reduce the impact of a single investment's performance on the overall portfolio.

Alternatives—like real estate, commodities, and private equity—offer a unique form of diversification because they're often not tied to the same market forces that affect traditional investments, like stocks and bonds. While stocks might dip due to market pressures, alternative investments can stay steady, providing stability when it's most needed.

This "low correlation" to the market is a big advantage. Since alternatives often respond to different factors than stocks or bonds, they tend to hold their value independently, even during stock market slumps. This independence from the usual market swings means that, when stocks or bonds experience volatility, alternatives can act as a cushion, helping to steady the portfolio. For example, in times when stocks might see a downturn, real estate or commodities might still hold their ground, which is reassuring for investors looking to weather uncertain markets.

There's another layer to this diversification benefit: risk-adjusted returns. This concept simply means that alternatives can help balance a portfolio's risk and potential return. By adding alternatives to the mix, an investor can create a blend of investments that offers a better balance of risk and reward than traditional assets alone. With a well-diversified portfolio that includes alternatives, investors reduce their exposure to market downturns, giving them a smoother path to growing their wealth without taking on unnecessary risk.

In short, alternative investments add resilience to a portfolio. They provide a layer of protection against market ups and downs, allowing investors to manage risk better and maintain steadier returns over time.

High Potential Returns

One of the most attractive features of alternative investments is their potential for high returns. Alternatives can offer access to asset classes that can yield significant growth. For instance, real estate is a classic example, whether it's residential buildings, hotels, storage facilities, or commercial spaces, real estate has long been known for delivering solid returns over time.

For investors who may not be able to buy and manage physical property, alternatives like real estate investment trusts (REITs) or private real estate funds make it possible to benefit from this market without needing to own property directly. Investing in these options lets people unlock the potential of rental income, property value growth, and diverse real estate profit streams - all without the headaches and hassles of being a landlord.

Beyond real estate, alternative investments also include assets like private lending, which can offer attractive returns. In this setup, investors lend money to businesses or individuals, often through private funds or peer-to-peer lending platforms. These loans can pay high interest rates, rewarding investors with strong returns in exchange for taking on more risk than they would with traditional bonds.

Other private assets, like equity in private companies or venture capital funds, can also provide substantial returns. These investments typically support small to mid-sized companies or startups that have strong growth potential but might not yet be listed on the public stock market. If these companies succeed and grow, investors in these private assets can see large payoffs over time, as the value of their shares or stakes increases.

However, with high potential returns comes the concept of the risk-return tradeoff. This depicts that while alternative investments often offer the potential for better returns, they also come with greater intensity of risk. For instance, investing in a new business through venture capital can be very rewarding if the company succeeds, but there's always the chance it could fail, leading to a loss.

Similarly, private lending might yield high interest payments, but there's a risk that borrowers may default, especially during economic downturns. Because alternatives can be riskier than traditional stocks or bonds, they are generally recommended as a smaller part of a portfolio, helping to balance potential rewards with a level of caution.

Ultimately, alternatives can provide a pathway to higher returns that aren't as readily available in the stock market. By diversifying into real estate, private lending, or other private assets, investors can access new income streams and potentially enhance their wealth in ways that go beyond the limits of public stocks.

Inflation Hedge

Alternative investments offer an effective way to guard against inflation, which gradually decreases the purchasing power of money over time. When inflation rises, everyday costs like food, gas, and housing increase, which can slowly eat away at the value of your savings. Traditional investments like savings accounts or certificates of deposit (CDs) often offer fixed returns that don't keep pace with inflation, especially when inflation rates climb.

However, alternative investments, particularly real estate and commodities, have built-in features that help them retain or even grow in value when prices rise. This makes them a popular choice for those looking to protect their wealth against the erosion of purchasing power.

Real estate is one of the most commonly used alternative investments for inflation protection. Property values and rental income tend to increase as inflation rises. For example, rental property owners can raise rents to match rising costs, providing an income stream that grows with inflation.

Over time, this income can help offset the higher expenses that come with inflation, making real estate an asset that doesn't just hold its value but often appreciates. This appreciation, combined with potential rental income, allows real estate to serve as a natural inflation hedge. So, while inflation may put pressure on traditional investments and cash holdings, real estate often thrives, helping investors maintain and grow their wealth.

Commodities, like gold, oil, and agricultural products, are another powerful tool for hedging against inflation. When inflation rises, the cost of goods and raw materials often follows, which in turn drives up the value of commodities. Gold, for instance, has long been considered a "safe-haven" asset because it tends to increase in value when other assets lose purchasing power.

Oil and agricultural products also benefit from inflationary trends, as rising costs of production and demand push their prices higher. For investors, holding commodities can mean benefiting from this price increase, which provides a buffer against inflation's impact on other parts of their portfolio.

In contrast, traditional low-yield investments like CDs and savings accounts are less effective in high-inflation environments. CDs might provide a fixed rate of return, which can seem stable, but that stability often fails to keep up with rising costs. For example, if inflation is at 5% and a CD is offering a 2% return, the real purchasing power of the returns is actually shrinking, leaving investors with less buying power over time.

On the other hand, alternatives like real estate or commodities typically have returns that rise alongside inflation, making them a far more resilient choice in these economic conditions.

While traditional investments struggle to keep up with inflation, alternatives adjust to the changing economy, helping investors protect their wealth and retain purchasing power. For those concerned about inflation's impact, incorporating alternatives can be a strategic way to build a portfolio that thrives, no matter how the economic landscape shifts.

Tax Advantages

A standout perk of alternative investments is their potential to unlock powerful tax advantages not found with traditional assets. For non-IRA investors - those investing outside retirement accounts - certain alternative investments can be structured to significantly reduce the tax burden on returns, allowing them to keep more of their gains. Unlike stocks and bonds, which are often taxed as ordinary income or short-term capital gains, many alternatives are designed to provide a more favorable tax treatment, which can make a big difference in long-term growth.

A key tax benefit of some alternative investments lies in the use of K-1 statements instead of traditional 1099 forms. A 1099 form typically reports income as taxable in the year it's earned, which means the investor has to pay taxes on that amount immediately. However, many alternatives—particularly those in private real estate or certain limited partnerships—issue K-1 statements instead. K-1s report income differently, often categorizing part of the income as a return of capital.

This is a crucial distinction because a return of capital is not taxed in the year it's received. Instead, taxes are deferred until the investment is sold or fully paid out, allowing investors to delay their tax payments and keep more of their earnings compounding over time. This deferral can be especially helpful in preserving cash flow, as it allows the investor to reinvest returns without immediately losing a portion to taxes.

Another advantage of alternative investments is the potential for long-term capital gains taxation. Contrary to ordinary income, which is taxed at the individual's full tax rate, long-term capital gains (applied to investments held for more than a year) are taxed at lower rates, typically 15% or 20% depending on income level.

Many alternative investments are structured to generate long-term gains rather than short-term income, meaning investors pay less in taxes on their profits. This is particularly beneficial for high-income investors, who face high ordinary tax rates on other forms of income. With lower capital gains taxes on alternatives, these investors can enjoy higher after-tax returns, boosting the overall yield of their investments.

For high-income earners, alternative investments offer even more tax benefits that make them an appealing choice for tax efficiency. These investors often face steep taxes on traditional income sources, especially if they're earning wages, dividends, or interest that are taxed at their full income rate.

By diversifying into alternatives that provide lower-taxed capital gains or use K-1 structures to defer taxes, they can create a more efficient income stream. This structure allows them to maximize their returns without incurring excessive tax penalties, which is necessary for building wealth over time. For those in higher tax brackets, these strategies provide a path to smarter, more tax-efficient investing.

In summary, alternative investments can offer a range of tax benefits that help investors reduce, defer, or even lower the rates on their tax obligations. With more of their earnings in hand and less lost to immediate taxes, investors in alternatives can boost their portfolios and grow their wealth more efficiently. These tax benefits are a strong draw for high-income and non-IRA investors who want their money to work smarter and grow faster over the long haul.

Cons of Investing in Alternatives

It's not possible for anything to stay purely on the positive side – almost everything we have around has both pros and cons, and alternative investments are no exception. These alternatives can be exciting because they promise something different, a chance to earn in ways that don't depend on the same ups and downs as the stock market. While they offer unique opportunities, they also carry a set of challenges that can make them complex and, at times, risky and unpredictable.

Alternative investments often need a special level of knowledge to fully understand and manage. Figuring out their true value isn't always simple, and predicting how they'll perform can be tricky. For some people, this adds to the excitement, but it also means that these investments can be complicated. You need to go in with careful planning, patience, and sometimes a readiness to deal with surprises. The potential is definitely there, but it's important to approach these opportunities with a clear understanding of what's involved.

Illiquidity

Illiquidity is one of the biggest challenges with alternative investments and a factor that makes them quite different from traditional assets like stocks or bonds. Liquidity simply means how easily you can buy or sell an investment to access your money. For example, stocks are highly liquid; you can sell them almost instantly on the stock market and have cash in hand quickly. But alternative investments often don't work that way. They can be much harder to convert to cash, which means your money could be tied up for longer periods—sometimes years.

This illiquidity can become even more of an issue when unexpected events happen in the economy, like the COVID-19 pandemic or periods of high-interest rates. During times like these, many people find themselves unable to sell their alternative investments, even if they need the money urgently.

Imagine someone with a large share of their money in real estate properties or private equity. If an economic downturn hits, selling a property or cashing out of a private equity fund isn't quick or easy. Properties, for instance, may sit on the market for months, or even years, if the economy is struggling. Private equity investments often come with strict holding periods, where you have to wait a certain number of years before you can sell.

During COVID-19, for example, many alternative investments were frozen, meaning investors had no option to sell even if they needed the cash. When interest rates are high, buyers might also be less willing to invest in certain types of assets, like real estate, which can make it difficult to sell without taking a big loss.

Because of this, it's often recommended to limit alternative investments to about 30% of your overall portfolio. This rule of thumb helps to protect you in case you need quick access to cash. By keeping most of your money in more liquid investments, you can have peace of mind knowing you'll still have accessible funds if something unexpected happens.

Diversifying this way can help you enjoy the potential benefits of alternatives without putting you in a tight spot if you suddenly need liquidity. It's all about finding a balance between growing your wealth and staying flexible with your finances.

Higher Fees

Higher fees are no doubt a defining feature of alternative investments, and grasping how they work is key to making smart choices. While traditional investments like stocks and bonds typically have simple fees - often just a small annual percentage or flat rate, alternative investments come with a more complicated fee structure. One common setup is known as the "80/20 split."

Here, the investment manager takes a 20% share of the profits, leaving the remaining 80% for the investor. This structure is typical in hedge funds and private equity funds, where the manager's fee is directly tied to how much profit they generate. So, if the investment performs well, the manager is rewarded, which can make investors feel that their interests are aligned.

In some cases, alternative investments also include something called a "preferred return." This is a minimum return that managers agree to deliver to investors before they take any share of the profits. For instance, a preferred return of 8% means that the investment must earn at least 8% before the manager can claim their 20% cut of additional profits.

The preferred return is intended to protect investors, ensuring they receive a certain level of return before any fees are taken out. However, suppose the investment does poorly and doesn't meet the preferred return threshold. In that case, the investor may get some protection, as the manager won't receive their profit share until that minimum is reached.

Compared to traditional investments, these fees might seem high, but they're often justified by the potential for higher returns and tax advantages. For example, certain alternative investments offer more favorable tax treatments, such as lower rates on long-term gains or tax deductions through real estate depreciation.

These tax benefits can make a big difference in the net returns that an investor receives, potentially offsetting the higher fees. Additionally, alternative investments generally require more hands-on management and expertise, which adds to their costs.

The managers involved often have specialized knowledge and networks that give them access to unique opportunities, such as buying into exclusive real estate deals or private companies that aren't available to the public. This expertise can come at a price, but for some investors, the potential gains and tax benefits make the higher fees worth it.

In short, while higher fees might initially seem like a downside, they often reflect the added value, complexity, and potential rewards that alternative investments bring to the table. Understanding these fees is essential, so you know what you're paying for and can decide if it aligns with your financial goals.

Complexity

Alternative investments are often more complicated than the usual stocks and bonds you might be familiar with. We might agree to the fact that public markets are simple and straightforward—just buy or sell shares with a few clicks, however, alternatives usually need a lot more understanding.

Things like private equity, hedge funds, real estate, or collectibles aren't traded publicly, and figuring out their value isn't always easy. Since these investments don't have the same level of transparency as stocks, it can be hard to know exactly what you're investing in and how it might perform in different economic situations. This complexity can make alternatives less accessible for everyday investors who might not have the time, resources, or expertise to navigate these complicated markets.

If you want to get into alternative investments, it's significant to take the time to educate yourself and do your research. It's not just about finding a good deal - it's about understanding how these investments work, the risks involved, and what kind of returns you can expect.

Doing your homework helps you choose investments that align with your financial goals and how much risk you're willing to take on. Even experienced investors often turn to experts for advice when it comes to alternatives because the market can be tough to understand. The more you learn, the more confident you'll be in your investment choices.

At this point, Registered Investment Advisors (RIAs) become very essential. These are professionals who assist you in understanding and managing the complexities of alternative investments. They have a fiduciary responsibility, meaning they are legally required to act in your best interest, not their own.

This is especially important with alternatives, where the risks and rewards can be harder to predict. An RIA can help you understand the ins and outs of these investments, weigh the pros and cons, and make sure you're not jumping into something risky without fully understanding it. Their expertise could make all the difference between a smart decision and getting lost in the details of alternative investment structures.

So, if you're thinking about diving into alternatives, don't try to go it alone. It's important to do your research, seek professional help, and make sure you really understand what you're getting into. With the right education and guidance, you can better grasp the concept of alternative investments and possibly unlock new opportunities for your financial future.

Higher risk

When the market faces a disruption, like an economic downturn or unexpected crisis, alternative assets may take longer to adjust. This delay in response can leave investors in a tough spot, especially if they need to access their funds quickly. Plus, the lack of transparency in some of these investments makes it harder to get clear information about how they're performing during these times of uncertainty. Take the 2020 pandemic, for example. It shook the global economy, and many alternative investments, especially in real estate and industries like hospitality, took a massive hit.

A hidden hazard of alternative investments lies in the risk of fraud and mismanagement, where murky oversight and lack of regulation can turn potential gains into major losses.

Because many of these investments aren't publicly traded, they don't face the same level of scrutiny as more traditional assets. This can lead to situations where unscrupulous individuals or poorly managed funds take advantage of the lack of oversight. Ponzi schemes, for instance, are more common in alternative investments, where new investor money is used to pay returns to earlier investors instead of generating real profits.

These scams can continue for years, hiding under the radar until it's too late for many investors. Even if fraud isn't involved, mismanagement can still be a major risk. If the team behind an alternative investment isn't doing their job properly, or if they're not transparent about how things are going, you could end up losing money or being left in the dark about the true value of your investment.

That's why working with experienced professionals who can perform thorough due diligence is so important when considering alternative investments. It's easy to get excited about the potential for high returns, but understanding the risks is what makes sure that you don't get caught off guard.

Professionals with expertise in alternative investments know what to look for, whether it's assessing the management team's track record or evaluating the investment structure itself. They can help you avoid falling into traps and ensure that you're investing in opportunities that align with your goals. They also know how to spot red flags, like a lack of transparency or poor financial practices, and can steer you away from investments that might be too risky.

There are many examples of alternative investments going wrong, often due to a lack of transparency or fraudulent behavior. One of the most famous cases is the Bernie Madoff Ponzi scheme, where thousands of investors lost billions of dollars after Madoff's firm was exposed as a massive fraud. Madoff had promised high returns, but in reality, the money from new investors was being used to pay off old ones. The scheme went on for decades, and many people didn't realize they were being scammed until it collapsed.

Another example is the 2008 financial crisis, where a lot of real estate-related alternative investments failed due to poor management and misleading valuations. Investors who had poured money into real estate funds or mortgage-backed securities found themselves with assets that plummeted in value when the housing market crashed. These examples highlight just how important it is to be diligent, work with trusted professionals, and thoroughly vet any alternative investments before committing.

If you do not want to step in the mud of risks, it's essential to approach alternative investments with caution. Make sure to research thoroughly and consult with experts who can clarify the more challenging aspects for you. Taking the time to understand what you're investing in and who's managing it can help protect you from potential losses and ensure that you're making choices that support your long-term financial goals.

Importance of Due Diligence and Professional Guidance

When you're dealing with alternative investments, it's easy to get swept up in the promises of high returns and unique opportunities. But here's the thing: without solid due diligence, all that glitter might just be fool's gold. This is where Registered Investment Advisors (RIAs) step in as your personal detectives. They don't just take things at face value; instead, they dig into every corner of an investment.

They look beyond the flashy pitches to the nitty-gritty details, examining the company's management structure, financial foundation, and even the past performance of similar investments. It's like an investigative mission to find out if the opportunity is as good as it sounds, or if it has any hidden traps.

With this level of scrutiny, RIAs give their clients peace of mind, acting as the guardians who separate genuine opportunities from risky gambles. Thanks to this process, clients can now enter into the world of alternatives with confidence, knowing someone's got their back.

Now, let's talk about spotting red flags. Imagine you're eyeing an investment that's promising you sky-high returns with zero risk, sounds amazing, right? Well, that's exactly the kind of promise that should make you raise an eyebrow. In finance, high returns without risk sounds like a fantastic idea but it's mostly mythical.

RIAs know that when something sounds too good to be true, it usually is. Another red flag? Strange tax perks. If an investment is claiming tax benefits that seem way better than what's typical, it might be worth taking a closer look. It could be a hint that things aren't as straightforward as they seem. Knowing these red flags helps investors avoid pitfalls and protects them from getting burned by questionable investments wrapped up in shiny packaging.

One major perk of working with a fiduciary advisor is that they're required, by law, to put you first. In contrast to other typical advisors, who might be influenced by commissions or personal gain, fiduciaries are all about doing what's best for you, plain and simple. They take the time to understand what you're looking for, your financial goals, and your risk tolerance, and they make recommendations with that information in mind.

It's not just about finding an investment that "works"; it's about finding the investment that's truly right for you. They'll tell you what fees to expect, point out any potential conflicts, and explain their thought process in a way that's straightforward and honest. With a fiduciary, you know you're getting the whole picture, with no hidden motives or surprises.

This makes a huge difference when you're looking at alternative investments that are often less transparent than traditional options. Working with a fiduciary advisor gives you peace of mind, knowing that you're not just getting any investment but one that's been carefully vetted and chosen with your best interests in mind.

It's honestly all about finding that sweet spot - a balanced approach. You want to look at the upsides, like the chance to diversify your portfolio and maybe even get some impressive returns, but don't ignore the risks lurking beneath the surface. By weighing these factors, you're putting yourself in the best position to make smart, informed choices.

Just giving you a good rule of thumb: keep it reasonable. It's tempting to go all-in when something new and promising catches your eye, but the core element here is moderation. Most experts recommend limiting alternative investments to a small chunk of your portfolio. This way, you can enjoy the potential perks without putting too much of your money at risk. Think of it like a spice, just the right amount can add some flavor, but too much can easily overpower the dish.

And, finally, let's not forget the importance of professional guidance. With alternatives, you're dealing with complex, at times, high-stakes choices that can be challenging to manage independently. Having an advisor in your corner, especially one who knows the ropes, can make a world of difference.

They can help you see beyond the shiny promises, spot any red flags, and guide you toward choices that align with your goals. So, as you begin exploring the realm of alternative investments, remember: balance, moderation, and the right professional support can make all the difference in turning these unique opportunities into a solid part of your financial future.

Chapter 5: Exploring Alternative Investments: Risks, Rewards, and Strategies

In recent years, the world of investing has seen a noticeable shift. Traditional asset classes like stocks and bonds, which once stood as the foundation of most portfolios, are now being complemented - sometimes even overshadowed, by alternative investments. This growing interest in non-traditional avenues can be attributed to a variety of factors: a volatile stock market, low interest rates, and an increasing desire for diversification and higher returns. As more investors begin to explore these alternative options, one thing becomes clear: there's no turning back. The appeal of alts isn't just a passing trend but a reflection of a changing investment sphere that acknowledges the need for balance and flexibility in today's unpredictable world.

However, as exciting as the promise of alternatives may be, it's essential to recognize that venturing into this territory requires more than just enthusiasm. The allure of high returns and unique opportunities is real, but so are the risks that come with them. This is where due diligence becomes absolutely crucial.

Due diligence refers to the process of thoroughly investigating and assessing a potential investment, business deal, or individual before making a decision. It's a way to gather all relevant information to make an informed, well-rounded choice.

Before diving into alternative investments, it's vital to take the time to fully understand the asset, its market dynamics, and how it fits into your broader investment strategy. Due diligence isn't just a formality - it's the foundation of smart investing. It ensures that you're making informed decisions that align with your financial goals and risk tolerance.

In short, while the growing interest in alternative investments is well-deserved, it must be tempered with a strong sense of caution and responsibility. As you explore these non-traditional options, remember that success doesn't come from jumping on the bandwagon; it comes from a deliberate, informed strategy backed by thorough due diligence. Only by doing the homework can you uncover the true potential of alternatives and integrate them into your investment plan effectively.

Private Credit: The Road Less Traveled

Imagine a world where access to capital isn't constrained by the rigid structures of banks or financial institutions. What if traditional credit scores and income statements didn't dictate your financial possibilities? This is private credit for you - a unique solution for borrowers who don't fit the mold of a "typical" applicant. For those who find themselves locked out of conventional financing options, private credit can offer a lifeline.

The Alternative Lending Landscape

Private credit represents a departure from traditional banking systems, providing an alternative source of funding for those who may not have access to regular credit channels. Think about individuals with unconventional income streams - freelancers, contractors, or entrepreneurs whose paychecks fluctuate month by month. They may find themselves ineligible for a bank loan, as banks often prefer borrowers with stable, predictable income. Similarly, small businesses or LLCs, particularly those in their early stages or without long-established credit histories, may struggle to secure financing from traditional lenders.

Private credit lenders, however, are willing to take on this challenge. They step in where conventional banks hesitate, offering loans to those who may otherwise be left out in the cold. The allure for borrowers? A chance to secure the funds they need, regardless of their credit score or lack of financial history. For investors, the appeal lies in the opportunity to earn a premium return by stepping into the space where traditional banks fear to tread.

Risks and Rewards: The High Stakes of Private Credit

On one hand, the higher interest rates - often ranging from 11-12%, are a clear draw for investors. These returns significantly outpace traditional investments like bonds or savings accounts, making private credit a potentially profitable source of income for those willing to tackle its complications.

But this higher yield doesn't come without its risks. Investors in private credit are often dealing with borrowers who don't have the solid financial standing that traditional banks would demand. These loans tend to come with higher interest rates to compensate for the additional risk, but the potential for default or late repayment is more pronounced.

Moreover, long-term holding is often a necessity, particularly for real estate-related investments. In this space, borrowers may be looking for financing that spans five to seven years, depending on the development cycle of the project. While this extended horizon can offer substantial rewards, it also means that investors may be in for the long haul before they see returns on their investment.

It's a game of patience. For those willing to wait, the reward is often substantial. For those hoping for a quick turnaround, the waiting period may seem like an eternity. But in private credit, time isn't just a factor - it's the source of the investment.

Drawbacks: When Transparency is Limited

One of the most significant challenges comes from the lack of transparency in borrower financials. Unlike traditional bank loans, where lenders have a clear picture of a borrower's creditworthiness through standardized reports, private credit investments can be a bit murkier. Many borrowers, particularly those with non-traditional incomes or businesses without a well-established credit history, may not have the financial documentation or credit scores that investors can rely on to gauge their ability to repay.

This lack of visibility can create difficulties for both borrowers and lenders. Borrowers may find themselves needing to navigate more complicated application processes to prove their worth, while lenders may be forced to make subjective judgments based on the borrower's business model, assets, or potential rather than hard data.

Moreover, the absence of a standardized credit system in the private credit space can make it challenging to gauge risk accurately. Without the familiar metrics and guidelines of traditional lending, each private credit deal stands on its own, requiring careful evaluation and a strong sense of trust in the borrower. This lack of uniformity increases the complexity for investors who may be used to the consistency of more traditional forms of credit. It's a space where due diligence is not just important; it's essential.

Venture Capital: The Gamble of Innovation

In a world where every new app, every groundbreaking tech company, and every life-changing product is born from an idea, someone has to take a chance. Enter venture capital, the bold, high-stakes world where investors place their bets on the next big thing before it's even a proven concept. It's the financial equivalent of putting your money behind a dream, with the hope that it becomes the next Facebook, Uber, or Google. But with the glory comes the risk, and venture capital is not for the faint of heart.

The Allure of High Rewards

Venture capital is built on a simple, yet powerful premise: the possibility of massive returns from an emerging business. The reward is high - think early-stage investments in tech startups or disruptive industries that have the potential to redefine markets and rake in millions (or billions) in returns.

This unique form of investment focuses on businesses with promising growth potential but little to no established history. For many, the thrill lies in the idea of being part of something revolutionary - backing the next big tech or health innovation before it hits the mainstream.

Here's the catch: for every success - every unicorn startup that soars - there are numerous failures. Venture capitalists invest in a portfolio of ideas, not just one. They spread their resources across several startups, knowing that most will fail. But they take this gamble because one successful venture can completely offset the losses from the others. It's the kind of risk that only those who understand the industry can afford to take, and it's the nature of the game: failure is inevitable, but it's the home runs that keep investors coming back for more.

The Risks: Failure is the Reality

A typical venture capital fund is diversified across several startups or ventures. Many of these startups will never make it past their first few years, and some may never make a profit. In fact, a common pattern in the venture capital world is that one massive success will offset several failures.

The potential for failure is high, especially in the early stages of a startup's development. External factors - such as market shifts, regulatory changes, or sudden shifts in consumer behavior - can dramatically alter the system of a company. Even the best-laid business plans can weaken when faced with the unpredictable nature of the world.

There's also the internal risk. If a startup's leadership changes or if the company pivots in a direction that investors didn't foresee, it could cause unforeseen consequences. A strong management team is critical in ensuring that the investment stays on course, but changes in leadership can lead to an entirely different direction, creating further uncertainty for investors.

For Whom Is Venture Capital Suitable?

So, who should be playing in the venture capital space? The average investor - someone looking for a steady return and less volatility - should probably stay away. The level of risk associated with venture capital is just too great for most people. It requires a deep understanding of the startup world, a sharp eye for emerging trends, and the stomach to ride out the inevitable bumps that come with this high-risk, high-reward setting.

This type of investment is most suitable for those who have both a high-risk tolerance and specific expertise. The individuals who thrive in venture capital often have years of experience in a particular industry and can spot emerging trends that others might miss. They have the know-how to evaluate the potential of a startup, even when that potential has yet to be fully realized. These investors are not just betting on the business model; they are betting on the people behind it and the innovations they bring to the table.

Venture Capital's Mainstream Rise: A Double-Edged Sword

As the world becomes increasingly familiar with the idea of venture capital, more and more investors are looking to get in on the action. What once seemed like an exclusive domain for tech tycoons and industry insiders has become more mainstream, as venture capital finds its way into everyday investment portfolios.

However, as venture capital grows in mainstream acceptance, the risks have not changed. In fact, some might argue that they've only increased as more players enter the market. The rise of crowdfunding platforms and the ease of access to venture capital funds have democratized the opportunity, but they've also made it harder to distinguish the truly promising startups from the fleeting ideas that are unlikely to survive.

While the prospect of getting in early on a hot new idea is tempting, the risks remain very much the same as they were before the field became more accessible. It's still a high-stakes game, and while some will strike it rich, many more will watch their investments disappear into the ether.

Green Energy and Impact Investments: Shaping a Sustainable Future

The promise of green energy and impact investments is to create a space where every dollar you invest contributes to the betterment of the planet. It is where sustainability and profit connect with each other. These are the investments that target socially responsible businesses—those working to preserve the environment, provide clean energy, and support communities. From solar power to forest preservation, these investments offer the chance to generate returns while also tackling some of the world's most pressing challenges.

Investors in this sector typically focus on companies or projects that prioritize the environment, renewable energy, and social good. Think solar farms, wind energy, and sustainable agriculture - industries that are not only growing but have the potential to reshape the world in a way that matters.

Beyond the promise of returns, these investments align with a growing global shift toward sustainability. More and more, individuals and institutions want to ensure their investments are part of the solution, not the problem. It's no surprise, then, that the green energy sector is booming, with governments and organizations worldwide making commitments to reduce carbon emissions and invest in renewable energy solutions. As the world's appetite for green energy increases, so too does the potential for profits.

Tax Breaks and Liquidity

One of the main attractions of investing in green energy is the potential for tax advantages. Governments, eager to support the transition to renewable energy, often provide significant incentives - whether through tax credits, subsidies, or grants. These incentives are designed to lower the cost of entry for investors and make green energy more attractive.

However, the flip side of these incentives is the lack of liquidity. Unlike more traditional investments, green energy and impact projects don't always offer a clear exit strategy. Most investments in this space are long-term, requiring years of commitment before seeing returns. The money is tied up in a project, and unless there's a major market shift or acquisition, the opportunity to withdraw funds may be limited. For investors seeking flexibility, this can be a significant drawback.

Additionally, these investments often lack the market transparency seen in more mainstream assets, making it difficult for investors to know exactly when or how they can cash out.

The Challenges: Political Winds and Changing Structures

When it comes to green energy and impact investments, the political climate plays a pivotal role. A shift in government leadership or policy priorities can have a significant impact on the profitability of green energy ventures. Take, for example, a sudden change in administration. A new government may roll back environmental regulations, reduce subsidies, or prioritize other sectors, leaving green energy projects vulnerable to sudden downturns.

What's more, political volatility isn't just a matter of national elections. Global climate policies, shifting attitudes towards climate change, and fluctuating government support for renewable energy can all affect the long-term viability of these investments. Investors who are banking on a smooth transition to a green economy could find themselves facing unexpected challenges if the political landscape changes.

Recently, some investors in green energy projects have found themselves locked out of their investments due to changes in the investment structure or corporate reorganization. As these projects evolve or grow, they sometimes shift from private to public offerings, change business models, or alter their funding structures in ways that leave early investors with little recourse. This lack of liquidity and changing project dynamics means that, in some cases, investors can't access their funds as anticipated.

Infrastructure Investments: Building Foundations for Long-Term Wealth

Picture this: A steady stream of income flowing from assets that you know will stand the test of time. Infrastructure investments - particularly those in commercial real estate and 1031 exchange-based ventures - offer just that. These are the types of investments that build wealth quietly but steadily, providing a solid foundation for financial security in the long run.

The Backbone of Long-Term Wealth: Commercial Real Estate and 1031 Exchange

When we talk about infrastructure investments, we're talking about tangible, long-lasting assets that are not only reliable but also growth-oriented. Think commercial real estate: office buildings, industrial parks, retail spaces, and even warehouses. These are the types of properties that businesses lease for years, ensuring a reliable stream of rental income. As cities grow, so does the demand for commercial spaces, making this type of investment one that can weather the storms of economic fluctuation.

Another powerful tool in the infrastructure investment world is the *1031 exchange*. This allows investors to defer taxes when selling a property, as long as the proceeds are reinvested into another similar property. It's a mechanism designed to keep your money working for you - without the immediate tax hit that could otherwise slow down your wealth-building strategy. The beauty of the 1031 exchange is that it allows you to grow your portfolio without being bogged down by the usual tax consequences. Instead of selling an asset and losing a chunk of the profits to taxes, you can roll those funds into the next investment, essentially compounding your returns in a way that other investment types can't match.

The Advantages: Tax Benefits and Stability

One of the standout reasons investors flock to infrastructure investments is the tax benefits. We've already touched on the power of the 1031 exchange, but there are other advantages that make these investments attractive. For example, when real estate is transferred through inheritance or a sale, the stepped-up cost basis can save substantial tax dollars. The stepped-up basis means that the asset is reassessed at its current market value rather than the original purchase price, significantly reducing capital gains taxes when it's passed on to heirs. This tax break can be a game changer for those looking to create long-term generational wealth.

However, tax breaks are just the beginning. Infrastructure investments are often seen as a safer, more stable option compared to other, more volatile assets. The reason? These assets generally hold their value better during economic downturns. People still need commercial spaces for business, and they still need to store goods in warehouses. As such, rental income from these assets remains consistent. For an investor looking for long-term stability and lower risk, commercial real estate ticks all the right boxes.

Why Infrastructure Is a Solid Bet for Long-Term Investment

At the heart of infrastructure investments is the promise of reliable returns. They may not offer the high-flying excitement of venture capital or the quick gains of day trading, but they come with something just as valuable: stability. While stock markets may rise and fall, infrastructure assets tend to hold steady over time, making them an appealing choice for investors who want to build wealth without the constant concern of market volatility.

These investments are ideal for those who are patient and willing to commit to a long-term strategy. Over time, the value of the properties can appreciate, while rental income provides a steady cash flow. It's a perfect blend for those looking for less risk, stable returns, and a long horizon.

Art and Collectibles: Where Passion Meets Profit

Art and collectibles have long been the playground for passionate investors who view them not just as objects, but as tangible assets that can hold and even grow in value. Whether it's a rare sports card, a vintage toy, or a painting by a world-renowned artist, the allure of investing in these unique items lies in their rarity, quality, and emotional connection.

These investments are not just about the financial potential but also about the joy they bring to their owners. Yet, the line between art as a personal passion and art as a serious investment can be quite blurred. So, what does it mean to invest in these items, and how do you know if it's the right move?

When we talk about art and collectibles, we're talking about an investment in something physically present, unlike stocks or bonds. Whether it's an original painting, a limited-edition sports card, or even a rare vintage doll, these are items that you can touch, admire, and enjoy. They offer something intangible: a connection to history, to culture, and often to a part of your own identity. But beyond the sentimental value, there's a growing recognition that these items can also offer lucrative financial returns.

The key to the potential return lies in the rarity and quality of the object in question. Some collectibles - like a piece of Impressionist art or a first edition comic book- have been known to skyrocket in value over time. Others, such as classic toys or vintage sports memorabilia, continue to enjoy steady demand in niche markets. Nonetheless, the market for art and collectibles can be unpredictable, and trends come and go. What's in high demand today may lose its luster tomorrow, making timing and research crucial for success.

The Duality of Art as Investment and Hobby

One of the biggest appeals of investing in art and collectibles is that it's not just an investment—it's a hobby. Many collectors buy art or vintage toys not only with the hope that they will appreciate in value but because they love the items themselves. Owning a piece of history or something that speaks to you personally can make it feel less like an investment and more like an experience. It's this emotional connection that differentiates art and collectibles from other types of investments, adding a layer of enjoyment to the process.

However, the challenge lies in separating personal interest from investment strategy. When a hobby becomes an investment, the line between passion and profit can blur. A painting you've always loved may be worth more than you paid for it, but its true value comes down to whether it appreciates over time. Some collectors make their fortune purely by the market demand for rare items, while others hold onto their collections for personal pleasure, regardless of their future value.

For the investor who chooses to combine the two - passion and profit, this can create a unique opportunity: owning something that not only holds aesthetic and sentimental value but also becomes a valuable asset in the long term.

NFTs and the Changing Landscape of Art Ownership

Now, let's explore a recent game-changer in the art world: NFTs (Non-Fungible Tokens) and digital art. For centuries, traditional art has been about tangible, physical pieces -

paintings hanging in galleries, sculptures standing tall in museums, and limited-edition prints coveted by collectors. However, with the rise of blockchain technology, the concept of ownership in art has dramatically shifted.

NFTs have created a new form of art ownership, one that's digital and unique but can still carry significant value. They challenge traditional ideas of ownership and authenticity by turning art into digital assets that can be bought, sold, and traded online. These digital pieces, often housed on platforms like Ethereum, can range from pixelated artwork to virtual fashion or even interactive digital experiences. Each NFT is one of a kind, secured by blockchain technology, ensuring that no two can ever be exactly the same.

While NFTs have opened up an entirely new realm of possibilities, they have also raised questions about the future of art investment. The value of NFTs can be volatile, as the market for digital art is still maturing, but they've already proven to be a lucrative avenue for the tech-savvy investor.

Still, the risk remains: Is digital art a sustainable investment, or is it a fleeting trend? As the NFT market fluctuates and as the art world adjusts to the digital revolution, only time will tell whether NFTs will be the next big thing or simply a passing phenomenon.

Art as a Timeless Asset

Despite the challenges and the rise of digital alternatives, one thing stays true: art is a timeless asset. Whether it's physical art or digital creations, art has always been a reflection of culture, society, and human experience. Its value is intensely associated with the stories and history it carries.

Whether you're investing in a Picasso or a rare sports card, understanding the market, the rarity, and the demand for the item is crucial. And, of course, whether it's for profit or pleasure, the connection you feel with the piece will always be at the heart of the investment.

Structured Products: Predictable, Yet Not Without Their Flaws

In a world where unpredictability is often the name of the game, structured products stand as a ray of certainty for investors seeking a predictable path forward. Imagine knowing exactly when you'll receive returns, understanding the clear timelines of your investment, and having a structured roadmap laid out for you. Structured products, like structured notes, offer just that - predetermined maturity dates and terms that bring a sense of stability. While they may provide a sense of security, they're not entirely free from complications.

The Predictability Advantage

For those who prefer a more calculated approach to investing, structured products can be quite appealing. These investments come with clearly defined timelines, and often, a predetermined return rate. This kind of transparency can be invaluable to investors who prioritize certainty over potential higher, but riskier returns.

The idea is simple: you commit your money for a certain period, and at the end of that period, you receive your returns.

It's a straightforward system that can be especially useful in an environment where unpredictability reigns supreme, like the world of stocks or commodities. For investors seeking predictable outcomes, structured products offer a comfort level that many other forms of investment cannot.

However, it's important to remember that the degree of certainty provided by these products doesn't mean they are completely immune to external factors. The returns on these investments are still influenced by market conditions or other factors beyond the investor's control, and the structured nature of these products doesn't necessarily mean that the reward is always guaranteed.

The Limitations of Structure

While structured products do offer a level of certainty, they are not as commonly seen in the world of alternative investments. The world of private equity, hedge funds, and other alternative avenues tends to favor more flexible and varied approaches, which can often provide larger upside potential, though with higher risks. Structured products are typically less dynamic, tied to fixed rules, and influenced by external economic or market factors, which can limit the upside potential compared to more aggressive investment strategies.

Moreover, the market for structured products isn't always as liquid as more traditional investments, meaning that getting out early or making adjustments can sometimes be challenging. So, while structured products can provide predictability, they come at the cost of flexibility - making them better suited for those who are less focused on seizing opportunities and more focused on sticking to a plan.

Stability for the Right Investor

For those who value certainty, structured products can be a stable choice. The predictable return timelines can be particularly appealing for those nearing retirement or others who seek financial peace of mind without constantly worrying about the ups and downs of the market. These investments provide the reassurance of stability, with the added comfort of knowing exactly when to expect a return.

However, this stability comes at a price: the potential for missed opportunities in the ever-changing investment landscape. With less room for flexibility and adjustment, structured products may not be suitable for those who are comfortable with volatility or are in pursuit of higher-risk, higher-reward options.

Top Investment Options to Consider

Fee-Simple Real Estate Investments: If you're seeking a solid foundation for your portfolio with excellent tax advantages, fee-simple real estate could be the answer. These properties offer long-term stability and, when done right, provide excellent tax benefits such as deductions on mortgage interest and property taxes. They also offer the added benefit of tangible assets that can appreciate over time, making them a fantastic addition for investors looking for both security and growth. Plus, they provide consistent cash flow through rental income, which can further diversify your portfolio.

Conversion Strategies for Roth IRAs: For investors looking to optimize their retirement savings, considering conversion strategies for Roth IRAs can prove advantageous. By converting traditional IRAs to Roth IRAs, you can benefit from tax-free withdrawals in retirement, giving you the potential for a larger nest egg without the burden of taxes when the time comes. However, this strategy requires careful planning, as it could lead to a higher tax bill in the short term. But for those with long-term thinking in mind, it can be a wise decision to grow wealth without worrying about tax consequences in the future.

Preferred Stocks as Bond Alternatives: If you're looking for an income-generating investment with lower volatility than stocks, preferred stocks can be a solid alternative to bonds. They offer steady income in the form of dividends, similar to bonds, but with the added benefit of principal protection in case of liquidation. For those looking for an investment that combines the safety of bonds with the higher returns of stocks, preferred stocks strike a unique balance.

Riskier Investments to Avoid

Venture Capital: While venture capital offers the potential for high rewards, it's an area fraught with high risk and often uncertainty. Investments in startups or emerging businesses can result in substantial gains, but the failure rate is high, and many investors end up losing their entire capital. For those without the expertise to evaluate early-stage companies, it's advisable to steer clear of venture capital. Even experienced investors often find this area to be a bumpy ride, so unless you have a high-risk tolerance and a deep understanding of the startup domain, venture capital is one area where caution is recommended.

Unlicensed Private Placements: When considering private investments, it's necessary to ensure that they are properly licensed and regulated. Unlicensed private placements can be particularly dangerous, as they often lack the transparency and oversight needed to protect investors. Without regulatory frameworks in place, these investments are susceptible to fraud, and in the worst cases, investors can lose their entire investment. Always ensure that any private placements you engage with have been vetted, are properly licensed, and come from trusted sources. If in doubt, it's best to seek out investments with clear regulatory oversight to protect yourself and your assets.

Cryptocurrency: The Digital Frontier of Wealth

Cryptocurrency has emerged from the shadows of niche tech communities into the spotlight of global finance as a new asset class that defies traditional norms. Yet, as it gains mainstream acceptance, it remains a high-stakes gamble - at once promising and hazardous.

Over the past decade, cryptocurrencies like Bitcoin, Ethereum, and countless altcoins have grown from speculative ventures to widely recognized investment vehicles. Initially regarded with skepticism, these digital currencies are now seen by many as a legitimate alternative to traditional investments like stocks, bonds, and real estate.

What began as an experiment in decentralization has blossomed into a global movement, with cryptocurrency advocates touting it as a revolution that bypasses the constraints of traditional banking systems. With the increased acceptance among major corporations, institutional investors, and governments, cryptocurrency is slowly finding its place in the world of mainstream finance. But as we move further into this digital frontier, investors must tread carefully - because cryptocurrency is not for the faint of heart.

Risks: The Wild, Unpredictable Ride

Despite its growing influence, cryptocurrency remains one of the most volatile and unpredictable asset classes. Price swings can be dramatic, with values fluctuating by double-digit percentages in a single day. Unlike traditional markets, which have long-established regulations and protections, the world of cryptocurrency is largely unregulated. This lack of oversight presents a unique set of challenges for investors.

For one, the absence of government regulation means there is no safety net for investors in case of market crashes or fraudulent schemes. If an exchange gets hacked or a digital wallet is compromised, there are few legal recourse for reclaiming lost funds. The potential for fraud in the cryptocurrency space is still high, with scams ranging from Ponzi schemes to rogue exchanges disappearing overnight.

Additionally, the regulatory uncertainty around cryptocurrency is a lingering concern. Governments around the world are grappling with how to manage, tax, and regulate digital currencies. A sudden shift in policy, such as the imposition of strict regulations or outright bans, could dramatically impact the value of cryptocurrencies.

Prospects: A Digital Asset with Potential

For all the volatility and uncertainty, cryptocurrency does offer some compelling prospects. The mainstream acceptance of digital currencies continues to grow, with more investors and companies adopting them as part of their portfolios. The potential for an extended bull market remains strong, particularly as governments become more open to the idea of digital currencies. Some investors see cryptocurrencies as a hedge against inflation, similar to gold, especially in times of economic instability.

Moreover, cryptocurrencies could benefit from less stringent government oversight. Without the intervention of central banks, these currencies are free from traditional monetary policies like interest rate adjustments or quantitative easing. This gives them the potential to thrive outside the control of central authorities, which can be an attractive quality for investors seeking to diversify their holdings in ways that bypass traditional financial systems.

Cryptocurrency as a Portfolio Addition: Proceed with Caution

So, where does this leave cryptocurrency in the grand scheme of your investment strategy? While it may be tempting to go all-in on this rapidly growing asset class, the high-risk nature of cryptocurrencies means they should only make up a small portion of your portfolio. For those comfortable with the volatility and the uncertainty, allocating about 10-15% of your investment portfolio to cryptocurrency is a sensible approach.

This allocation allows you to tap into the potential for high returns without overexposing your portfolio to the wild swings inherent in digital currency markets. Cryptocurrencies should be seen as a high-risk, high-reward investment - ideal for those who have a high-risk tolerance and are prepared for the possibility of both significant gains and losses.

However, even if you are willing to embrace the potential rewards, it is critical to diversify your investment strategy. A well-balanced portfolio should still include more traditional investments, like stocks, bonds, and real estate, to mitigate the risks associated with the digital asset class. By keeping cryptocurrency to a manageable portion of your portfolio, you position yourself to capitalize on its growth potential while reducing the impact of its volatility on your overall financial health.

To sum up, it's important to really understand each type of investment, from real estate and private credit to cryptocurrencies and green energy projects. By knowing what you're getting into, you can make decisions that align with your personal goals and comfort level with risk. Remember, the best investment for one person might not be the right fit for another, so take the time to assess what works for you.

One thing to keep an eye out for is investments that don't have clear exit strategies or are too poorly regulated. It might be appealing to jump on an opportunity that promises high returns, but if you're unsure about how or when you'll be able to sell your investment, or if there's little oversight to protect you, it could end up being more trouble than it's worth. Always ask yourself: "What's the plan if things don't go as expected?" Investments that lack transparency or regulation can be risky, and it's important to approach them with caution.

Lastly, never hesitate to reach out for help from experts when you're making big decisions. Whether it's a financial advisor, an accountant, or an investment professional, consulting with someone who knows the ins and outs of the market can give you peace of mind. They can guide you in the right direction, helping you make informed decisions that best suit your needs and goals.

In the end, making smart investment choices is all about being informed, thoughtful, and cautious. With the right knowledge and advice, you can build a strategy that helps grow your wealth, all while staying in control of your financial future.

Chapter 6: Unlocking Wealth Through 1031 Exchanges and DSTs

For many real estate investors, the decision to sell a property comes with one looming obstacle: taxes. After years—sometimes decades—of managing tenants, handling repairs, and fielding those late-night plumbing calls, you might be ready to let go. But just when you're thinking about a smoother path ahead, the capital gains tax shows up like an unexpected toll booth on your retirement highway.

That's where the 1031 exchange comes in. Named after Section 1031 of the IRS Code, this strategy allows investors to sell one piece of real estate and roll the proceeds into another—deferring the capital gains taxes in the process. It's one of the most powerful tools in the investor's playbook when used correctly, and it's not just about taxes. It's about legacy. It's about simplifying life. And for many, it's about unlocking the wealth tied up in bricks and mortar and converting it into hands-free income that supports retirement or estate planning goals.

But here's the catch: the traditional 1031 exchange often just swaps one problem for another. Sell a triplex, buy a fourplex—you're still chasing tenants and managing maintenance. That's why more investors are turning to DSTs—Delaware Statutory Trusts—to take advantage of the 1031 exchange without the headaches of active property management.

In this chapter, we'll explore how 1031 exchanges work, why DSTs are rising in popularity, and what you need to know if you're thinking about transitioning from hands-on to hands-off real estate wealth. Whether you're downsizing your portfolio, planning your estate, or simply tired of unclogging other people's toilets—this chapter might change the way you think about real estate investing forever.

What Is a 1031 Exchange?

At its core, a 1031 exchange allows a real estate investor to sell an investment property and reinvest the proceeds into another qualifying property—all while deferring capital gains taxes. The concept is rooted in Section 1031 of the Internal Revenue Code, which permits this kind of tax-deferred exchange when certain conditions are met. It's not a loophole; it's a legally sanctioned strategy that encourages reinvestment and economic growth.

To qualify, the exchange must involve "like-kind" properties. That term often causes confusion, but it doesn't mean a duplex must be exchanged for another duplex. In IRS terms, "like-kind" simply means both properties must be held for investment or business purposes. You could sell a rental condo in California and exchange it for a strip mall in Texas or a medical office in Florida—so long as both are income-producing or held for appreciation.

There are some key rules to follow:

- **Identification Rule:** Once you sell your original property, you have 45 days to identify up to three potential replacement properties in writing.
- **Exchange Period Rule:** You must close on one (or more) of those identified properties within 180 days of the sale of the original property.
- **Qualified Intermediary (QI):** You're not allowed to touch the money in between. The funds must be held and transferred by a QI, who ensures compliance and paperwork.

If you miss these deadlines or fail to reinvest the full amount, you could be hit with a capital gains tax bill on the proceeds. Depending on your tax bracket, that could be 15%–20% federally, plus depreciation recapture and state taxes, potentially wiping out a significant chunk of your profits.

The beauty of the 1031 exchange is that you can continue exchanging properties over and over, deferring taxes each time. And if held until death, your heirs receive a step-up in cost basis, meaning they inherit the property at its current market value, completely wiping out deferred taxes.

In essence, the 1031 exchange isn't just a tool to delay taxes—it's a roadmap for building and preserving wealth over time. But while it's powerful, it also demands precision, timing, and expertise—which is why DSTs are starting to change the game for investors looking for something smarter, simpler, and stress-free.

Introduction to DSTs (Delaware Statutory Trusts)

Imagine being able to sell your real estate, defer taxes through a 1031 exchange, and still collect monthly rental income—without ever dealing with a tenant, a leaky faucet, or a 2 a.m. call about a broken heater. That's the promise of the Delaware Statutory Trust, or DST.

A DST is a legally recognized trust formed under Delaware law that allows multiple investors to hold fractional interests in large, institutional-quality real estate assets. These properties might include apartment complexes, medical facilities, distribution centers, or retail buildings—the kind of assets normally out of reach for individual investors. Each investor owns a beneficial interest in the trust, while a sponsor company—usually a professional asset manager—handles all day-to-day operations.

The DST structure is fully approved by the IRS for 1031 exchange purposes, which means you can sell your existing investment property and use the proceeds to purchase an interest in a DST—deferring capital gains taxes just as you would in a traditional 1031 exchange.

Here's how it differs from a standard 1031 exchange:

- In a **standard 1031**, you're exchanging one whole property for another. You maintain full control—and full responsibility.
- In a **DST 1031**, you're exchanging into a **fractional interest** in a trust that owns one or more properties. The DST, not you, holds title, manages tenants, collects rent, handles maintenance, and eventually sells the property.

This distinction is crucial. With a DST, you are truly passive. There's no property management, no decisions to make, and no need to fly across the country to inspect a roof. The sponsor takes care of everything while you collect distributions—usually monthly.

As for who qualifies: DSTs are typically available to **accredited investors**, meaning individuals with a net worth exceeding $1 million (excluding primary residence) or annual income over $200,000 ($300,000 if married) for the past two years. This requirement ensures investors understand the potential risks and are financially equipped to handle them.

The DST is not a new fad. It's a well-established legal structure, backed by the IRS Revenue Ruling 2004-86, and used by countless real estate investors seeking both simplicity and tax efficiency. For aging landlords, busy professionals, or families focused on estate planning, DSTs offer a way out of active ownership—without stepping away from real estate altogether.

Key Benefits of DSTs

For many investors, especially those nearing retirement or managing substantial property portfolios, the appeal of a Delaware Statutory Trust lies in one word: freedom. DSTs offer a way to remain invested in real estate without the physical, emotional, or logistical burdens of direct ownership.

1. Truly Passive Income: DSTs eliminate the hands-on headaches of property management. Investors don't field tenant complaints, oversee repairs, or deal with property taxes or insurance renewals. Those responsibilities are handled by the professional sponsor managing the trust. You simply receive monthly income distributions, often directly deposited into your account. It's real estate ownership, streamlined.

2. Consistent Monthly Distributions and Backend Appreciation: Most DSTs are structured to provide predictable monthly cash flow, backed by rental income from high-quality, stabilized properties. Whether the trust owns a distribution facility leased by Amazon or a chain of medical clinics, that income is passed through to investors. And when the property is sold—typically after 5–10 years—investors also participate in backend appreciation. In other words, you earn along the way, and you benefit when the asset sells.

3. Powerful Estate Planning Tool: One of the most compelling reasons families explore DSTs is for their estate planning advantages. Under current tax law, if an investor holds a DST interest until death, their heirs receive a step-up in cost basis. This means any deferred capital gains taxes vanish, and the property is inherited at its current market value. For investors with long-held, highly appreciated real estate, this can result in millions of dollars preserved for the next generation—tax-free.

4. Diversification Without Complexity: Large property portfolios—especially those built over decades—can be difficult to unwind without triggering a tax avalanche. DSTs allow investors to slice large exchanges into smaller, manageable pieces, distributing proceeds across multiple geographic regions, asset types, and tenants. An investor can exit a $10 million portfolio and reinvest in six or seven DSTs across industrial warehouses, grocery-anchored retail, and healthcare real estate—all without lifting a finger to manage any of it.

In short, DSTs take the core appeal of real estate—tangible assets, reliable income, long-term appreciation—and strip away the work, leaving only the wealth-building components. For many investors, it's not just a tax strategy; it's a lifestyle shift.

Common Property Types in DST Portfolios

DSTs aren't invested in fixer-uppers or speculative land plays. They're built around **institutional-quality real estate**—the kinds of properties you've likely walked past, driven by, or even used yourself without ever knowing it was owned by hundreds of investors through a trust.

- **Commercial Real Estate:** Many DSTs include **office buildings**, particularly those leased to **credit-rated tenants** like Fortune 500 companies or government agencies. These leases tend to be long-term and structured with triple-net terms, meaning the tenant covers taxes, insurance, and maintenance. This helps provide stable and predictable income to the trust.

Medical centers are also common. Properties leased to national health systems or specialty clinics offer resilience in all market conditions. The medical sector continues to grow regardless of broader economic trends, making it a **defensive anchor** in many DST portfolios.

• **Storage Facilities and Multifamily Units;** Self-storage facilities have quietly become one of the most reliable performers in real estate. High demand, low overhead, and steady cash flow make them ideal for DSTs, especially in urban or fast-growing suburban areas.

Multifamily units—such as apartment complexes—are also popular, offering built-in occupancy diversification and consistent monthly rent. These properties often sit in high-growth regions where housing demand remains strong.

• **Semiconductor and Specialty Buildings:** With the rise of advanced manufacturing, especially in the tech and energy sectors, some DSTs are now built around semiconductor facilities, research hubs, or data centers. These properties are often leased on a long-term basis to highly specialized tenants, locking in income for years.

• **Retail Centers with National Brands:** Retail properties included in DSTs are not the mom-and-pop strip malls of decades past. These are usually grocery-anchored shopping centers or free-standing buildings leased to nationally recognized brands like CVS, Walgreens, Starbucks, or Ralphs. These tenants provide brand-name stability, frequent foot traffic, and strong lease covenants.

What ties these properties together is their income-generating stability and professional management—ideal for investors seeking security, predictability, and minimal involvement.

Ownership Structure and Investment Size

DSTs aren't about buying the whole building—they're about owning a piece of the building, and doing so in a legally protected, professionally managed structure.

When you invest in a DST, you are purchasing a beneficial interest in a trust that owns the real estate, not shares in a company or a deed to a property. This structure is similar to a limited partnership, where the sponsor operates the property, and you, the investor, receive income and long-term gains.

• **Fractional Ownership, Full Advantage:** You may own just 2% of a $50 million medical complex, but your percentage entitles you to 2% of the income, tax benefits, and appreciation. Your name isn't on the title, and your responsibilities are nonexistent—but your return potential is very real.

• **Typical Investment Size:** DSTs generally require minimum investments between $100,000 and $500,000, with most investors allocating $1 to $3 million to take full advantage of the 1031 exchange rules and diversify across multiple trusts. Advisors often break a large real estate sale into multiple DST investments, pairing a $1.2 million multifamily DST with a $900,000 medical office DST, and so on.

This approach spreads risk across asset types, locations, lease lengths, and tenant industries. If one building sells slower or has a short-term vacancy, the others can still produce income—offering a cushion that a single replacement property rarely provides.

DSTs may not offer the control of owning a duplex down the street, but for many high-net-worth individuals nearing retirement or seeking hands-off income, they offer access to premium real estate with a fraction of the cost and none of the hassle.

Holding Periods and Liquidity Options

One of the first questions investors ask when considering a DST is: *"How long will my money be tied up?"* The answer depends on the strategy behind each trust, but in general, DSTs are not designed for short-term liquidity. They are structured to mirror the natural investment cycle of real estate—focused on steady income and long-term appreciation.

• **Standard Holding Period: 5–6 Years:** Most DSTs follow a 5- to 6-year holding cycle. This gives the sponsor time to stabilize operations, collect steady rent, and time the eventual sale for favorable market conditions. During this period, investors typically receive monthly income distributions, while the value of the asset (ideally) appreciates in the background.

Once the property is sold, the investor has two primary options:

1. Roll into another DST or qualifying property via a new 1031 exchange (and continue deferring taxes).
2. Take the cash and pay capital gains, depreciation recapture, and other applicable taxes.

• **Longer-Term DSTs and Partial Liquidity:** Some DSTs are structured for longer holds—up to 9 or 10 years. These often involve triple-net-leased commercial assets with stable tenants under long-term contracts. In a few select cases, the DST offers a partial early exit strategy through a loan structure. This mechanism allows investors to withdraw up to 90% of their invested capital after a specified period, using their original interest as collateral.

It's important to note that this structure doesn't eliminate your DST position; it simply offers limited liquidity while maintaining your investment's tax-deferred status. These early-exit options may come with interest rate considerations, depending on the lending market at the time of withdrawal.

- **Interest Rates and Appreciation:** Appreciation potential varies by asset class and market conditions. Medical office buildings in growing cities may outperform a suburban retail center, but both are still subject to cap rates, tenant performance, and macroeconomic forces. In low-interest-rate environments, cash flow from DSTs is generally higher, as borrowing costs for the underlying properties are reduced. When rates rise, distributions may tighten, but the principal preservation and backend appreciation often remain intact.

The key is understanding that DSTs are **not day-traded assets**. They're designed for investors seeking predictable, tax-efficient income with long-term upside, not for those needing quick access to funds.

Use Cases and Client Profiles

DSTs are not just theoretical tools—they solve very real problems for very real people. Over the years, certain investor profiles consistently emerge as ideal candidates for this strategy.

• **Elderly Investors Seeking Simplicity:** Picture a couple in their seventies who've spent the last 40 years managing a dozen rental properties. They're worn out. Their children live out of state. The idea of dealing with another broken boiler—or worse, a tenant lawsuit—is not just inconvenient; it's overwhelming. DSTs offer them a way to stay invested in real estate without being shackled to it. Monthly income still flows, but the effort required drops to zero.

• **Couples Managing Estate Transitions:** DSTs are also powerful tools for couples thinking generationally. A common situation: one spouse handles all the real estate decisions, and the other, often by choice, stays uninvolved. But what happens if the more active spouse passes away first? The surviving spouse may be left with a confusing portfolio they never wanted to manage. DSTs simplify the inheritance process by turning complex, hands-on assets into clean, passive income streams—and when held until death, heirs receive the step-up in basis, eliminating capital gains tax liability.

• **Owners of Large Commercial or Multifamily Holdings:** Another common case involves owners of high-value commercial buildings, triplexes, or multifamily developments. These properties may be worth millions, but managing them comes with a steep time and energy cost. DSTs offer an exit ramp. Instead of selling and taking a massive tax hit, these investors can transition their capital into multiple DSTs, maintaining income and growth potential without the baggage of direct ownership.

DSTs aren't a fit for every investor, but for those ready to reduce stress, increase efficiency, or plan for the next generation, they can be **transformative**.

Partial Liquidation and Cost Basis Considerations

One of the most misunderstood but strategically valuable aspects of 1031 exchanges—especially when executed through DSTs—is how they allow for partial liquidation and intelligent tax planning around cost basis.

When a property is sold, the IRS sees two potential sources of tax exposure:

1. The **original cost basis**—what the investor paid for the property, including capital improvements and depreciation adjustments.
2. The **appreciated value**—the gain in value since the property was acquired.

The key insight here is this: investors are allowed to reclaim their original cost basis, including documented capital improvements, tax-free. This withdrawal is not considered capital gains; it's simply getting your own money back.

Let's say you purchased a rental property 20 years ago for $500,000 and put $200,000 into renovations. If you sell it for $1.5 million today, your total investment basis is $700,000. You can withdraw that $700,000 at closing—take it in cash, put it in a savings account, or use it to buy a second home—and pay no capital gains tax on it. It's your principal, not a profit.

The remaining $800,000 in appreciation is what triggers capital gains taxes. However, by rolling that portion into a DST through a 1031 exchange, you defer those taxes indefinitely.

This approach is often referred to as taking some "boot" off the table. In IRS terms, "boot" is any portion of the sales proceeds not reinvested in like-kind property. The beauty here is that you can intentionally structure the exchange to take partial boot in the form of your cost basis and only defer the appreciated portion—giving you flexibility without triggering a massive tax bill.

For investors nearing retirement, this hybrid strategy offers the best of both worlds:

- **Immediate liquidity** for personal goals or expenses.
- **Long-term tax deferral** and passive income through DST investments.

It's a sophisticated move, but with the right guidance, it can be one of the most powerful wealth-preservation tools in the 1031 playbook.

Risks and Considerations

As appealing as Delaware Statutory Trusts may sound—and for the right investor, they can be a game changer—it's essential to approach them with a clear understanding of the trade-offs and limitations. DSTs are built for stability and tax efficiency, but they are not without risk, rigidity, or compromise.

• **Timeline Extensions and Market Uncertainty:** DSTs operate on long-term investment cycles, and while sponsors generally target 5- to 6-year hold periods, those timelines are not guaranteed. External factors—like inflation, interest rate spikes, or global events (think: COVID-19 pandemic)—can delay the sale of a property. For example, in 2020 and 2021, many DST sponsors paused exit strategies, waiting for market stability to return before liquidating properties. While monthly distributions continued in many cases, investors had to remain patient.

This highlights an important truth: you don't control when the DST sells the asset, and therefore, you don't control when your principal comes back.

• **Less Control Over Investment Decisions:** With DSTs, you are a passive investor—entirely hands-off. While this is a major draw for many people, it also means you relinquish decision-making authority. You can't choose tenants, renegotiate leases, decide to sell early, or make capital improvements. Those decisions rest solely with the sponsor.

This makes it crucial to work with reputable, experienced DST providers who offer transparency, communication, and proven performance. A good advisor will help you evaluate offerings and understand sponsor history, property metrics, and tenant reliability before committing.

• **Illiquidity and Exit Restrictions:** Unlike stocks, mutual funds, or even REITs, DSTs are illiquid. Once your capital is invested, it is locked in for the duration of the trust's hold period. You can't redeem shares, sell your interest, or exit early—unless a structured loan provision is offered (and even that is limited).

This structure reinforces the need to treat DSTs as long-term investments. They're ideal for wealth preservation and income generation, but they're not well suited for investors who may need emergency access to funds or want the ability to pivot quickly.

Final Thoughts

Delaware Statutory Trusts aren't for everyone—but for the right investor, they can represent a financial turning point. For landlords burdened by decades of hands-on property management, for aging couples concerned about what happens after one of them is gone, or for investors sitting on highly appreciated assets in high-tax states like California or New York, DSTs offer a rare combination of relief, reinvestment, and reward.

Those who benefit most from 1031 DSTs tend to fall into three overlapping categories:

- Investors seeking **passive income** without giving up real estate altogether.
- Families looking for **cleaner estate planning options** and capital gains tax elimination through stepped-up basis.
- Owners of **high-value properties** are ready to exit active management while preserving their wealth.

But just as important as the strategy itself is the person guiding you through it. This is where qualified financial advisors and 1031 specialists become indispensable. Advisors help clients navigate timing rules, avoid "boot" exposure, and ensure that the DSTs selected are diversified by property type, location, and tenant quality. They act as the bridge between complex tax law and practical implementation.

The end result? Investors go from owning a duplex down the street—with all its responsibilities—to holding fractional interests in stabilized, income-producing assets across the country. They defer capital gains, generate consistent cash flow, and preserve wealth for the next generation—all without answering a single tenant phone call.

In a world where real estate wealth can come with very real burdens, DSTs represent something rare: a graceful exit. Not an escape from the market, but an elevation within it—a shift from operator to investor, from stress to strategy.

www.ingramcontent.com/pod-product-compliance
Lightning Source LLC
LaVergne TN
LVHW022101200926
848481LV00003B/1018
* 9 7 9 8 3 4 9 5 7 6 3 6 2 *